HOW TO **MAKE MONEY** WITH YouTube

Earn Cash, Market Yourself, Reach Your Customers, and Grow Your Business on the World's Most Popular Video-Sharing Site

BRAD AND DEBRA SCHEPP

McGraw Hill

New York   Chicago   San Francisco
Lisbon   London   Madrid   Mexico City   Milan
New Delhi   San Juan   Seoul   Singapore
Sydney   Toronto

ISBN: 978-0-07-162136-6
MHID: 0-07-162136-9

How to Make Money with YouTube is no way authorized by, endorsed, or affiliated with YouTube or its subsidiaries. All references to YouTube and other trademarked properties are used in accordance with the Fair Use Doctrine and are not meant to imply that this book is a YouTube product for advertising or other commercial purposes.

Readers should know that online businesses have risks. Readers who participate in online business do so at their own risk. The author and publisher of this book cannot guarantee financial success and therefore disclaim any liability, loss, or risk sustained, either directly or indirectly, as a result of using the information given in this book.

McGraw-Hill books are available at special quantity discounts to use as premiums and sales promotions, or for use in corporate training programs. To contact a representative please visit the Contact Us pages at www.mhprofessional.com.

To our nieces, Elissa Sorkowitz Lejeune and Adina Sorkowitz Levin: When you were small we thought that you were brilliant, beautiful, and completely magical. Now that you're grown, we know it to be true!

CONTENTS

CHAPTER 4

CREATING YouTube VIDEOS   85

CHAPTER 5

PROMOTING AND DISTRIBUTING YOUR VIDEOS   119

CHAPTER 6

YouTube: YOUR NEW REVENUE STREAM   153

ACKNOWLEDGMENTS

Any book requires hundreds of hours of research and then hundreds of hours of writing. Although we've worked on many projects together in our years as writers, we've never been a team of only two players. There are always hundreds of people behind any project, and this one was no different in that respect. Where it was different was in how much fun it was to research. We've never laughed so hard while working! We've also rarely met a group of people who are so optimistic, creative, and energized about what they were doing. We're going to do our best to thank them all, but because we know we're bound to miss a few, please accept our apologies before we even begin. The Internet is vast, and YouTube is a big neighborhood, but we honestly feel that we leave this project behind with a whole corral of new friends. We wish all of you success.

First, we'd like to thank Aaron Zamost, Corporate Communications, YouTube, for his Johnny-on-the-spot help. Lynn Tornabene of Google was also there just when we needed her.

As for the YouTube experts: we'll start with Michael Buckley of the ever-entertaining, and addictive, *WhatTheBuck?!* Asa Thibodaux, you are truly a kind and funny guy. Here's the deal: if we're down to our last $10, and you tell us you're hungry, we're all going to Taco Bell! He's a dad who used YouTube to forge a whole new career against some pretty major odds, and then he was kind enough to share his experience with us. To Davide Ricchetti, a guitar-painting artist and a natural wonder, we'd like to say *grazie mille*. Thank you, Paul "Fitzy" Fitzgerald—a guy who seems to always be having fun and enjoying life. Paula Drum, vice president, Digital Tax Marketing, H&R Block, showed us that even serious tax types are into YouTube. David Mullings of Realvibez, you were always there when we had a question, and you may have taught us more than anyone about successful marketing on YouTube. Kipkay is one of the brightest stars in a galaxy of stars, and always willing to help, thanks Kip. Anuja Balasubramanian and Hetal Jannu were wonderful, and we only wish we lived close enough to them so we could invite ourselves for dinner. Watching their YouTube show, *ShowMeTheCurry!* made us stop for lunch every single time! Arnel Ricafranca of *Fitness VIP* showed us we had nothing to fear but his abs. TubeMogul's David Burch is one of the true pioneers of this new field, and Steve Hall of AdRANTs whose blog of the same name (AdRANTs, not Steve) is something your inbox will enjoy every day. Jon Hilner of the University of Alberta found fame with *Diagnosis Wenckebach* and showed that even overworked medical students just want to have fun on YouTube. Leah Nelson and Jay Grandin of GiantAntMedia.com, made us take a second (and third) look at how we shower. (Honestly, guys, where did you hide that camera to learn how we shower?) Marc Black created a video that gave Martha Stewart pause, and Bob Thacker, Senior Vice President of Marketing and Advertising at OfficeMax, blew away any preconceptions we may have had about "corporate types." The same is true for Michael Parker of Serena Software. (Magic really *can* happen in the IT department once that pocket protector comes out!) Dr. Steven Yarinsky, thanks for the advice about gaining exposure in a professional way on YouTube. Clearly your advertising needs no facelift. Thank you to George Wright of Blendtec, the *WillIt Blend?* guy who quickly saw how to mix up things in the sometimes staid world of advertising. Ben Relles of *Obama Girl* and barelypolitical.com fame, thanks, although, honestly, you made us wish we were about 20 years younger! We appreciated everything you did so much, that we're still willing to thank you.

Still more YouTube mavens include Ralph Lagnado and David Abehsera of the Woo Agency, just some of the grownups behind Fred's success. Also, thank you to Jamie Dolan, of Sonestaentertainment.com, Fred's business manager; Ryan Adler of Drumpr.com; Maisha Drexler of Acadian Ambulance; Prabhat Kiran; Fred Light; Amer Tadayon of Render Films; JohnScott Dixon of Semanticator; and Patric Douglas, CEO of Shark

Diver. Thank you to Chris Chynoweth of DropKickMonKey.com (Chris, you were a big help, but we implore you, please don't ever drop-kick a monkey), Paul D. Potratz Jr., of the ad agency bearing his name, Chrissy Coplet of Talking Goats Videos (no, we don't make this stuff up), and Alex Huff of Loudclick.net. Thanks go to "Steve" the Austrian Barber, Pablo D. Andreun of 5W Public Relations, and Shev from Metacafe who helped so much. Vimeo.com's Dalas Verdugo deserves our thanks, and so does Kristen Wareham of Yahoo!, MySpaceTV's Paul Armstrong, Scott Lorenz of Westwind Communications, and Mike Dunklee of Quicken Loans were great, and to Samara O'Shea, thanks for keeping alive the fine art of journaling and letter writing. Andrew Lipsman of comScore and Samson Adepoju, communications coordinator at eMarketer, thanks. Steve Metzmen, CollegeSupplement.com; Jeannine C. Lalonde, assistant dean of admission, University of Virginia; Susan Peters, Kodak; and also Peter Shankman of Help a Reporter; Taylor Davidson of TechCrunch, we appreciate your input.

A special thanks to our agents from Waterside Productions, Inc., Bill Gladstone and Ming Russell. You take all the stress out of the business part so we can get down to the writing part. We like the writing part much better, so we're beyond grateful to you.

At McGraw-Hill, we'd like to thank our editor, Knox Huston. You were a pleasure to work with, and you agreed so easily that we had a great idea. Just a hint, authors will always love you for that kind of thing. We'd also like to thank our editing supervisor, Daina Penikas, our copyeditor, Scott Amerman, and our proofreader, Suzanne Rapcavage, for making us look much smarter than we are.

A special thanks goes out to our kids, Stephanie, Andrew, Ethan, and Laurel. This started out being more their world than ours. They offered us their support and help as we completed this project, and they didn't show much resentment as we came to know more about it than they do! Finally, to Max and Mollie, thanks for making sure our desktops and printers were, as always, free from mice. It's hard to imagine what a completed manuscript would look like without its fair share of cat hairs.

INTRODUCTION

It isn't often that we get to witness a life-changing innovation. Our parents spoke of their first television sets with an enthusiasm those of us who grew up with the device couldn't quite appreciate. Honestly, did people gather in one house in the neighborhood just to watch Milton Berle? In many ways, the following generations have been extraordinarily fortunate. Not only did we see the arrival of the Internet and all that came with it—e-mail, instant messaging, online shopping, online banking, global positioning systems, just to name a few—but we've also seen the arrival of Web 2.0 technologies. Social networking and social media have changed the Internet almost as much as the Internet has changed us.

Thanks to YouTube and other social media sites, each one of us can take center stage and present our views of life to a worldwide audience. For the very first time, individuals have access to the same broad audience once reserved for major television networks and their wealthy advertisers. This is not to suggest that anyone can just pick up a camera and automatically gain the exposure and gravitas of, say, Walter Cronkite. But each of us can work in our own little corner of YouTube to create a following and an audience for our own particular view on life. Whether we go onto YouTube to spread a political message, promote our businesses, or share our humor (as everyone else seems to think we're funny), we've got the power within our own hands to change our lives through video on demand. Even Queen Elizabeth II has her own place on YouTube!

But, the question remains, can you make money with YouTube? The answer to that question is . . . YES. True, it all depends upon your definition of "making money." If you think that you've only actually made money when you've added dollars to your bottom line, then YouTube success may elude you at first. But if making money can also mean saving on advertising expenses and branding costs, then please stay tuned.

Throughout the pages of this book, we're going to introduce you to individuals and company representatives who are convinced that YouTube changed their lives. You'll meet comedians who now earn stipends as YouTube partners. You'll meet public relations officers who report more than 1,000 percent increases in their sales as a result of their YouTube presence. You'll meet sales and marketing executives from Fortune 500 companies who are now so smitten with the success they've realized on YouTube they may never plan another advertising campaign without it. You'll meet Fred, a 14-year-old farm kid who not only has an advertising agency working on his behalf but also retains a business manager who advises him and his family about what to do next. You'll meet stay-at-home moms who are supplementing their family's incomes and forging fascinating new lives for themselves. All these people had an idea and stuck with it long enough to learn how to make that idea profitable.

Now, this is not to say that you'll necessarily row your little boat down the River YouTube to guaranteed fame, fortune, and happiness. We've been at this profession a little too long to believe that we're privy to the next great get-rich-quick scheme. The path to success on YouTube is more like a winding estuary than a raging river. In addition to the success stories on the site, you'll find a whole lot of junk, but a lot of it is golden, too.

In the chapters that follow, you'll discover how to create a YouTube presence in the latter category. You'll get acquainted with the phenomenon that is YouTube, learn how both individuals and companies are using the site to achieve their goals, and explore the basics of how to produce a great video. Then, once you have your video posted to the site, you'll learn how to promote and distribute it so that it won't be lost in the tsunami of video that gets added to the site every day. Finally, you'll find out about potential revenue-sharing sources for you through YouTube, and you'll learn about other online video-sharing sites that might prove to be at least as profitable for you as YouTube is.

All along the way, you'll discover the fun and enthusiasm that marks YouTube and its contributors. You may have to go a long way to find a group of people more energized and enthusiastic about the work they're pursuing.

It's been a great deal of fun to research and write this book. It's our fervent hope that you'll find it to be a great deal of fun to read it.

Brad and Deb Schepp
www.bradanddeb.com

YOU TOO CAN BE A YouTube STAR!

When Sarah Silverman appeared on then boyfriend Jimmy Kimmel's talk show in early 2008, she had a video to share with him and his viewers. She introduced it by explaining this was the perfect moment to share some personal news with the late-night talk show host. The film rolled, and our unsuspecting host learned that Sarah Silverman was sleeping with Matt Damon! For those of us who turn in much earlier than Jimmy and Sarah, we were still able to catch the video, and even watch it endlessly. It appeared on ABC.com and it went viral after appearing on YouTube, spreading like any viral infection, from one viewer to another. Matt and Sarah happily sang and danced through several minutes of raucous video announcing their newly consummated relationship. Sarah went on to garner an Emmy nomination for her video song, and Jimmy followed up with a YouTube video of his own, announcing that he, in turn, was bedding Ben Affleck! Naturally, that video quickly went viral too, receiving millions of views as everyday folks logged on to see Jimmy's friends, including Robin Williams, Harrison Ford, and Cameron Diaz help him tell Sarah that he was well over her and her indiscretions.

Combined, these two videos have been viewed more than 10 million times. But, you may ask, and with good reason, what's that got to do with you and your business goals for YouTube? If you're like us, you don't happen to hang out with the likes of Robin Williams, Harrison Ford, or Cameron Diaz. We're pretty sure Sarah, Matt, Jimmy, and Ben don't even know we exist. But, one thing we all have in common is the potential to strike it big on YouTube. We're here to tell you that 99 percent of the most successful people on YouTube are like us, not the Hollywood elite. "Average" people and companies are finding fame and fortune on YouTube with some regularity, and everyone has an equal shot, thanks to this amazing phenomenon.

Since its founding in 2005 (yes, that's right, it's that recent), YouTube has revolutionized the way people all over the world share information, entertainment, education, and advertising. Between 1948 and 2008, the three major television networks in the United States produced 1.5 million hours of programming, according to professor and YouTube video lecturer Michael Wesch. YouTube users, he's said, have produced more than that in the last six months! In fact, YouTube estimates that 13 hours' worth of video gets uploaded to the site every *minute*. More important than the statistics, however, are the demographics behind the statistics. For the first time ever, programming has been taken away from the major players with the big money and put squarely in the hands of every person who decides to create and post a video. You may not have the fame and glory, yet, but you have the same shot at exposure that once was reserved only for those rare few people destined to become stars.

Throughout the pages of this book, you'll meet dozens of individuals and company representatives who have found ways to make YouTube work for them. Whether they have launched businesses or refreshed corporate images, they have used YouTube to open doors they would never have dreamed of just five years ago. Now that these doors are open, our lives as video consumers and producers will never again be the same.

YouTube AND YOU

Before you pick up that camera and start creating your own videos, consider some of the ways YouTube has altered the landscape of our everyday lives. You'll get some background, navigate around the site, and receive a little bit of philosophy as you are introduced to people who have paved the way for the rest of us to achieve success on YouTube. Not only is YouTube a wonderful source of entertainment but it is also a major breakthrough in the way we share our experiences. Most important of all, YouTube can be a powerful business tool. That's no doubt why you picked up this book—to learn how you can step onto the site and use it to make money, directly or indirectly, for yourself or your company.

YouTube defines itself as "a community where people are entertained, informed, educated, and inspired through the sharing of video." Figure 1-1 shows you just what to expect from YouTube's home page. More than 200 million unique visitors arrive at this page each month from all over the globe, according to the company. Of those, 68 million are from the United States.

FIGURE 1-1: YouTube's HOME PAGE PROMISES FUN AS SOON
AS YOU ARRIVE.

Those 68 million U.S. viewers are evenly distributed across the country. They split just about equally between male and female viewers. The overall demographics skew somewhat young, with 56 percent of registered users falling between the ages of 18 and 34—a prime advertising demographic. Kick in the fact that 73 percent of viewers say they don't mind the discrete advertising that now accompanies some videos, and you've got a willing and prime market. They recognize that advertising is the means for keeping the site free to users. As if this news weren't good enough for those of us looking to enhance our businesses, 68 percent of YouTube users report they have purchased something online in the previous three months. We told you this would be exciting!

YouTube corporate is a tad coy and only releases the most general numbers about site usage, but this is what the company was saying as this book was being written:

People are watching hundreds of millions of videos a day on YouTube and uploading hundreds of thousands of videos daily. In fact, every minute, ten hours of video are uploaded to YouTube.

We're willing to bet that as you read this, the numbers are even more impressive. So, how do you find a way to distinguish yourself in this ever-increasing buzz of creativity? That's a very good question without an easy answer. Let's start with a reassuring story so you can see that, although it may not be simple, it is possible to start with nothing but a good idea and make that idea grow into a genuine YouTube phenomenon. Say hello to Hetal Jannu and Anuja Balasubramanian, shown in Figure 1-2. You may not know them, but tens of thousands of people who log on for *ShowMeTheCurry!*, their weekly cooking show on YouTube, do.

FIGURE 1-2: *SHOWMETHECURRY!* STARS HETAL JANNU AND ANUJA BALASUBRAMANIAN, TWO HOMEMAKERS TURNED FILMMAKERS, THANKS TO YouTube.

ShowMeTheCurry!

Hetal Jannu and Anuja Balasubramanian, two 30-something homemakers from suburban Dallas, Texas, are probably much like many of the moms you know in your own neighborhood. Both interrupted their careers to launch their families. Both found themselves looking for something interesting to do once the kids were in school full time, and both share a love of and expertise with Indian cuisine. When the two friends decided to give the world of TV cooking a try, they found a home right on YouTube.

"ShowMeTheCurry.com's debut was on YouTube," explained Hetal recently. "At the time, it was the one sure way to reach a worldwide audience. We had a Web site, but to be page-one-ranked on any search engine is nearly impossible for newcomers. How would anyone find us? Our strategy was to become popular on YouTube and funnel the traffic to our Web site from there." It's a strategy that's proven to be very successful. In just over a year the two have more than 120 videos on YouTube, and they're doing quite well earning money through ad sales and sponsorships. They have relationships with partners including Google, Advertising.com, and BlogHerAds, to name a few. They have more than 1,700 subscribers to their YouTube channel, and they're having a ball along the way.

When they began, Hetal and Anuja had one thing going for them. They were both devoted and experienced cooks. Although neither was formally trained as a chef, both had grown up learning the techniques of Indian cuisine and gaining a lifetime's worth of tasty recipes. They decided to focus on two target audiences. "We targeted beginner cooks with exact, tried, and tested recipes and foolproof methods," said Hetal. "We also targeted seasoned cooks with healthy alternatives to traditional Indian food and time-saving tips." Hetal explained that the pair tries very hard to release videos consistently: "If you have one or two videos and take a break, your viewers will forget about you."

This is just one of the many lessons these two have learned in the year or so since they began. At first, they'd selected Saturdays as filming days, and they appointed their husbands as the cameramen. It didn't take too many hectic work-filled Saturdays spent with the kids entertaining themselves before Hetal and Anuja realized that to be successful, they were going to have to learn to work independently. They set about learning how to film, edit, produce, and advertise their YouTube show themselves. Editing was their real challenge. Neither had ever edited video before, so their first efforts involved a sharp learning curve. But they dedicated themselves to learning the software required for the task, and today they're quite comfortable with every aspect of the job at hand.

These days Hetal and Anuja get to work as soon as the kids leave for school, and the cooks are busy until the youngsters come home at the end of the school day. The two friends often finish up details after the kids have gone to bed. In just over a year, the show's stars have built a stable full of successful videos and a loyal fan following. Their Web site is thriving, and Hetal expects that eventually their enterprise will earn them the equivalent of two full-time salaries. As the brand grows, Hetal believes revenues will increase through product placements within the videos. From doing video production to setting up search engine optimization to generating revenues, these two "ordinary" housewives have struck out for fame and fortune right in their own kitchens, doing what they both love, and loving their lives on YouTube. Maybe they are not so ordinary after all!

Are You the Next "Cewebrity"?

Ralph Lagnado and David Abehsera of the advertising firm Woo Agency have coined a word to describe Hetal and Anuja: they're "cewebrities." Ralph and David know a thing or two about the subject, because they are from the agency that represents one of YouTube's biggest stars: Fred. You'll learn a lot more about Fred in Chapter 2, but we were so captivated by the term these two came up with that we wanted to introduce you to it right away.

Cewebrities like Hetal and Anuja are a new type of celebrity created through the video sharing made possible on YouTube. Armed with a good idea, a special niche, and a willingness to both work hard and learn, people like these two stay-at-home moms have crafted their very own path to success. They're making money by doing what they love best while still taking care of their families. If they achieve some fame and recognition for their hard work, that's even better. What they've accomplished has never before been possible. But, Hetal and Anuja aren't alone. To whet your appetite, we'll give you glimpses of more individuals you'll meet throughout this book.

More YouTube Cewebrities

Asa Thibodaux is a rising young comedian who is actually able to support his family through his YouTube videos. Many people have aspired to live the life of a stand-up comedian, but of the many thousands who set out on that path, how many actually ever earn a living? Most of them are comedians by night and waiters by day, but Asa is managing just fine, thanks to YouTube.

Michael Buckley writes, records, edits, and manages his own YouTube show, *What the Buck?!*. His show is currently one of the most popular channels on YouTube, attracting more than 230,000 subscribers and 4.5 million views. He brings his own snappy, funny, and gay spin to celebrity gossip. "My goal is to do something," says Michael. "I need people to watch me who think they never liked gay people. I try to also get people [to watch] who say they don't like celebrity gossip." Michael still works his day job, although he admits he probably doesn't need to. He just likes the work and its benefits.

Ben Relles launched his Web site barelypolitical.com with the debut of *Obama Girl*. He used a production team to film a hot girl as she danced through the streets and subways of Manhattan singing about her crush on Barack Obama. Ten million YouTube members couldn't resist her, and 22,000 people commented on that first video. As we write, there are more than 30 other *Obama Girl* videos on the site.

When we spoke with Fred Light, he was doing very well in spite of the real estate slump causing panic throughout the rest of the country. Location, location, location has a new meaning now, and this savvy producer of real estate videos is so successful and skilled that his properties routinely appear on the first page of relevant Google search results within three hours of his posting them!

A QUICK GUIDED TOUR OF YouTube

The people behind YouTube have worked hard to make the site easy to navigate and use, so you won't need much handholding. As you can see from Figure 1-1, it's not too hard to find a video that interests you right from YouTube's home page at www.youtube.com. First, you'll see a row of videos being watched *right now*. Next, you're offered a glimpse at the promoted videos, and finally a group of featured videos take up a lot of that first page. If nothing there entices you, and we're betting that something will, you can click on hyperlinks for More Featured Videos, Most Viewed, Most Discussed, and Top Favorites. It may take a new user several sessions just to move beyond the home page!

All the while, calling to you is the empty search box that just begs you to put in your own topics of interest to locate videos that will appeal just to you. Just about any keyword(s) you can think of will pull up related videos. Through the pull-down menu you can specify whether you want to search videos or channels. The featured channels are like cable channels in the sense that their focus is narrow and they're devoted to a theme. For example, as we mentioned, Michael Buckley, of the popular *What the Buck?!* show has his own channel. So do record companies, political and news organizations, conventional networks such as Comedy Central and CBS, and a lot of YouTube born-and-bred stars besides Michael. We'll describe many of these success stories throughout this book.

After you do a search, you can sort the results by relevance, date added, number of times it was viewed, and the rating YouTube members assigned it. Once you watch a video, finding similar videos is a snap. Related videos appear to the right, as well as other videos from that source.

As you follow the tabs along the top of what YouTube calls the watch page, you'll find tabs for video, channels, and community. The Video and Channel tabs are self-explanatory, but take a closer look at the information that resides behind the Community tab. Clicking that tab will take you to the screen shown in Figure 1-3. Here you'll find Contests that are mostly operated by businesses. (We'll look at those very closely in Chapter 5.) You'll also find Groups, where people of like tastes can gather and share. Finally, you'll find Community Help Forums. Here you can come to ask questions, meet other YouTube users, and read about experiences others have had with the site. This is a great place to stop as you work to join the YouTube community.

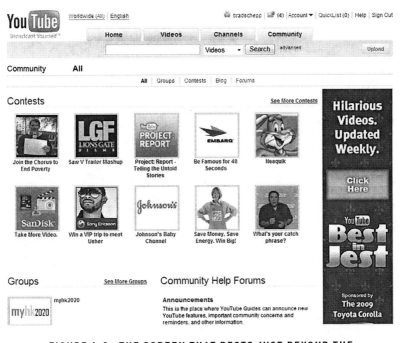

FIGURE 1-3: THE SCREEN THAT RESTS JUST BEYOND THE
COMMUNITY TAB OF YouTube's HOME PAGE.

And now to the subject of signing up for YouTube. You can spend countless hours browsing and enjoying YouTube without registering with the site. But, if your goal is to become a member of the YouTube community—and, for your purposes, it must be— you need to sign up (or, as YouTube refers to it, "Create an Account"). Once you do, you'll be able to comment on videos, subscribe to your favorite channels, and collect your favorite videos into your own little corner of the site. Fortunately, signing up is quick, painless, and free. Figure 1-4 shows the form you'll need to complete to officially sign up with YouTube, and create your own account. Simply complete this form, select a username and password, supply some general demographic information, and agree to the terms of service. With the next click of your mouse, you're all set to start exploring the entire YouTube community as an official YouTuber.

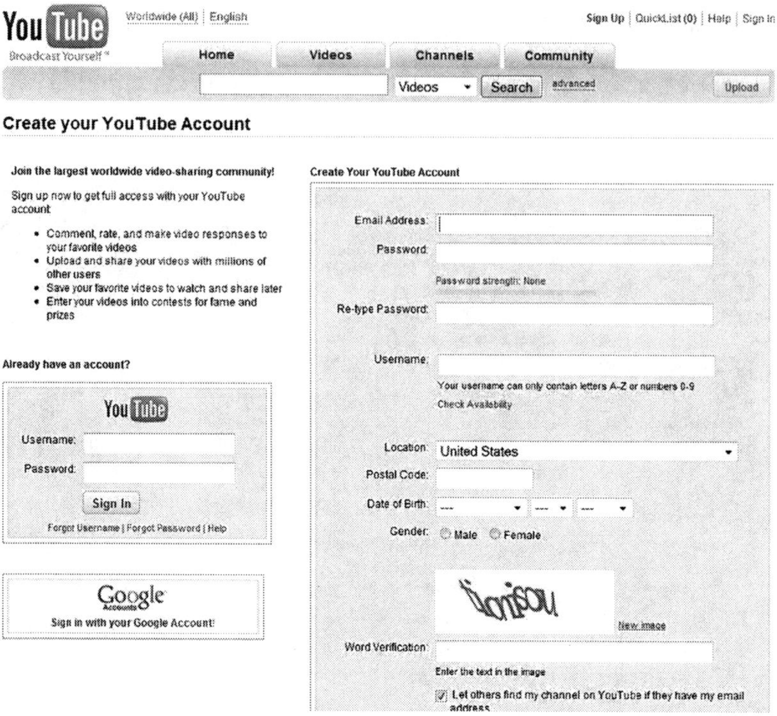

FIGURE 1-4: USING THIS SCREEN YOU WILL QUICKLY AND EASILY CREATE YOUR OWN ACCOUNT ON YouTube.

A YouTuber is the default account type you're assigned when you first create an account. Once you've gotten your account established, you can change that account type to better reflect what you hope to do on YouTube. You can select from Comedian, Reporter, Musician, Director, or Guru.

Types of YouTube Accounts

No matter what type of account you have, you can participate fully as a member of the YouTube community; that is, you can upload videos, comment on videos, create a playlist, and share videos. Each of the specialized accounts, however, differs in the way you can brand yourself through your Channel page. Your Channel page is where you organize your YouTube information such as your own favorite videos, your subscribers, the videos you've uploaded, and the personal information you provided when you set up your account including where you're from, what you do for a living, where you went to school, and so on.

Here are the major differences among the accounts:

Comedian: This account type is for people who do stand-up, parody, satire, or sketch comedy. As a Comedian, you'll be permitted to add a custom logo, provide a more extended profile, give show date information, and link CD purchases to your Channel page.

Director: This one is for show creators and personalities who entertain and inform on YouTube. If you select this type of account, you'll be able to list customized performer information that will appear on your Profile page, including such things as your style and your influences. As with the Comedian account, you can show your personality with the use of custom text and graphics on your Channel page.

Guru: You'd select this channel if you were planning to upload how-to types of videos that reflect your expertise, whether that is cooking, creating videos, knitting, or any other area you feel competent to advise others about. Gurus have the same ability to customize their Channel pages as Directors and Comedians.

Musician: This is the place for bands, singers, songwriters, and even representatives of record labels. Anyone involved in the world of music will want to select this type of account. Once you've done that, you'll be able to include a custom logo on your Profile page and list genre, tour date information, and links to CDs you've bought.

Reporter. Get ready all you scribes out there! Select this account type if you write for a print or online publication, or are a broadcast journalist. You don't even need press credentials. Individuals can join professional journalists in reporting and commenting on local, national, and international news. As a reporter, you can create a Channel page that describes your own particular beat. You can explain your influences and perspectives, and list your own favorite news sources. If you can't get enough politics and news, this could really be the place for you to call home!

When you first sign up on YouTube, you'll be a basic YouTuber. If you decide you'd rather sign up for one of the more specific account types, you'll get your chance in several ways. The very last screen you'll see as you complete the

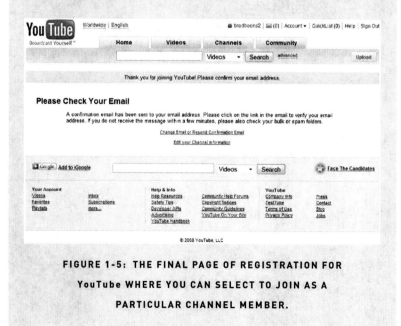

FIGURE 1-5: THE FINAL PAGE OF REGISTRATION FOR YouTube WHERE YOU CAN SELECT TO JOIN AS A PARTICULAR CHANNEL MEMBER.

sign-on process, shown in Figure 1-5, directs you to check your e-mail for your registration confirmation. But, as you can see, it also offers you a hyperlink to edit your channel information. Now that you've completed registration, you're free to alter your status.

If you're already a registered member, and you have a basic YouTuber account, don't worry. Simply click on your Account hyperlink at the top of most pages, then channel info, and finally change channel type. As you can see in Figure 1-6, from there you can select an account you feel more specifically identifies you and your YouTube goals.

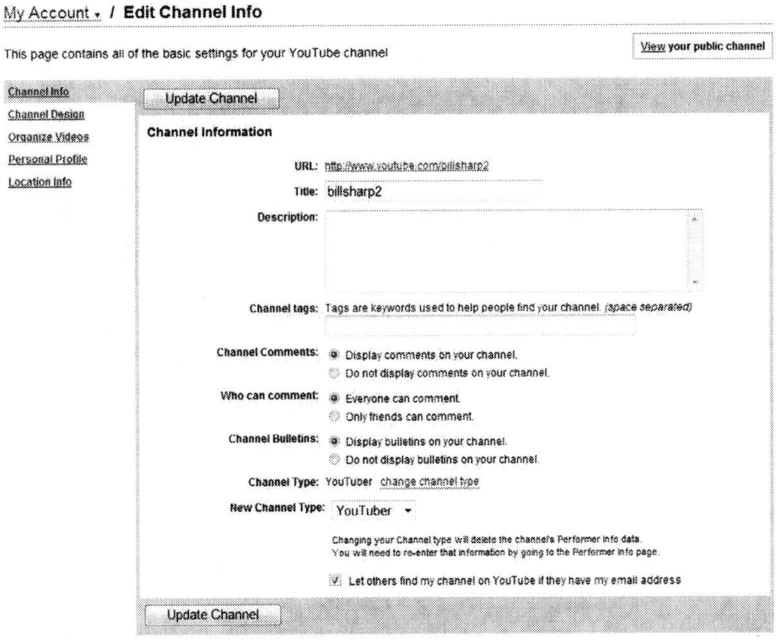

My Account ▾ / **Edit Channel Info**

This page contains all of the basic settings for your YouTube channel   View your public channel

Channel Info   Update Channel
Channel Design
Organize Videos   **Channel Information**
Personal Profile
Location Info   URL: http://www.youtube.com/billsharp2

                                            Title: billsharp2

                                      Description:

                                   Channel tags: Tags are keywords used to help people find your channel. (space separated)

                               Channel Comments: ● Display comments on your channel.
                                                  ○ Do not display comments on your channel.

                                Who can comment: ● Everyone can comment.
                                                  ○ Only friends can comment.

                               Channel Bulletins: ● Display bulletins on your channel.
                                                  ○ Do not display bulletins on your channel.

                                   Channel Type: YouTuber change channel type

                               New Channel Type: YouTuber ▾

                                                  Changing your Channel type will delete the channel's Performer Info data.
                                                  You will need to re-enter that information by going to the Performer Info page.

                                                  ☑ Let others find my channel on YouTube if they have my email address

          Update Channel

FIGURE 1-6: THE SCREEN YOU'LL USE TO CHANGE YOUR ACCOUNT TYPE IF YOU ARE ALREADY A YouTuber.

There is one more type of YouTube account, but that one is clouded in some mystery and intrigue. YouTube content creators, who have gained some popularity and therefore have some clout, may apply to become YouTube partners. (Or YouTube may make the first overture and extend the invitation directly.) YouTube partners share in the revenue that is generated from advertising that runs against their videos. YouTube, understandably, is somewhat secretive about exactly what makes a content creator ready for partnership and how much money is involved in such an arrangement.

Here are the basic criteria YouTube says you must meet to become a YouTube partner:

- You create your own original videos that can be streamed online.

- You own or have legal permission to use and make money from the audio and video content that you upload—no exceptions!

- You regularly upload videos that thousands of YouTube users watch.

- You live in the United States, Canada, the United Kingdom, Japan, Australia, Ireland, Germany, France, or Brazil.

We spoke with many such partners throughout our research for this book, but not one of them felt free to answer any questions about revenue-sharing arrangements that are part of their deal with YouTube. We respectfully declined to pump them too hard for answers, because a commitment to nondisclosure is just that, and we are honorable writers. So, we'd love to tell you more specifics, but instead we'll say this: keep working, think of great new ideas, post your videos, and someday, perhaps, with a little luck and a lot of hard work, you'll gain all the information you need about YouTube partnerships directly from YouTube itself.

YouTube: Yours to Explore

No doubt you'll want to explore YouTube for yourself. That's the great fun of YouTube: one click leads to the next, and before long you've found yourself wandering all over the site, exploring and discovering. Here are some helpful suggestions to set you out to find your own way.

YouTube's Handbook Is Simple to Find

YouTube provides a simple and fun handbook right on the site that's full of information for both finding videos you might enjoy and creating your own videos. It's a great first stop for new YouTubers, because it answers your questions succinctly and some of those answers are actually in the form of video responses to your questions. Just click on the Community tab to get to it.

YouTube's Glossary Can Help

YouTube provides a glossary on the main Help Resources page shown in Figure 1-7. If you come across a term that doesn't mean anything to you, hop on over to Help Resources, click on the Glossary link, and the glossary will be there ready with a definition.

What Can You Do with Those Videos Once You've Found Them?

Once you start finding your way around YouTube, you're bound to come across videos you enjoy or feel compelled to share. That's the value of this social medium. The millions of videos on the site are there to be viewed, shared, and enjoyed by the YouTube community. As you go about taking your place within that community, be sure to comment on, share, and rate the videos you see. After all, you probably benefit from the ratings and comments. And, you must have opinions of your own. In subsequent chapters, as we discuss different ways to make money and gain exposure for yourself or your company, you'll find us often

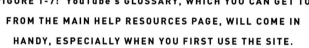

FIGURE 1-7: YouTube's GLOSSARY, WHICH YOU CAN GET TO FROM THE MAIN HELP RESOURCES PAGE, WILL COME IN HANDY, ESPECIALLY WHEN YOU FIRST USE THE SITE.

returning to this community theme. Let's get started with some of the most basic ways to share videos and interact with other YouTubers. As you might have already guessed, YouTube makes the process simple.

Share Your Treasures

The first tab under each video box is the Share tab. Click here to e-mail the video or post it to social networks such as MySpace and Facebook. The more people who share a video, the more likely that video is to go viral, spreading just like last winter's flu, but without the misery, all across the Internet. If you hope to have viral videos of your own, and that's what most of us hope for, you're going to want to be sharing other people's videos first. By doing that, you can get acquainted with the process of sharing, and help set down roots in the community.

The other tabs below each video window allow you to add a video to your favorites list, create playlists of your favorite videos, and flag videos you find to be inappropriate for the site. Just for fun, search for "Ethan Laughing." You'll find an adorable little guy playing a silly game with his dad and laughing a most appealing baby laugh. We're not the only ones who have enjoyed this video, called "Laughing Baby." There were more than 18 million others when last we checked. Not only that, but AIG Investments used part of it for a television commercial, which is also posted to YouTube. (Search for "AIG Laughing Baby Ethan Commercial.") No doubt it's likely there's something in baby Ethan's college fund from that AIG deal, and from the laughing baby ring tones for sale on the Web site www.LaughingBaby.com! Of course, we added the original video to our list of favorites. Next, search for "Hahaha." The first video to appear features a most charming little character caught in hysterics by some silly sound his dad is making. More than 59 million viewers enjoyed this one, and more than 160,000 rated it. Now, you can see where we're going with this. Not only do we want this as a favorite too, but we're going to create a playlist. That way, whenever we're feeling down, we can take a few minutes to remember how important it is to laugh. Our new playlist is entitled, of course, "Laughing Babies." As for the flagged videos, if you do find one, and it's likely you eventually will, simply click on the Flag tab. YouTube staffers do investigate every flagged video, and those found to violate the site's Community Guidelines will be removed.

Another way to support the people behind the videos is to use the Subscribe button. On the right corner of every video Watch page is the member information about the video contributor. For example, Figure 1-8 shows you the page for a video from Hetal and Anujah of *ShowMeTheCurry*! Next to the thumbnail of the two, you'll find how long they've been on YouTube, how many videos they currently have on the site, and a hot button that allows you to

FIGURE 1-8: SUBSCRIBING TO A CHANNEL IS AS EASY AS CLICKING ON THE SUBSCRIBE BUTTON IN THE CONTRIBUTOR DETAIL BOX.

subscribe to their channel. Once you click that Subscribe button, you'll receive an e-mail any time they post a new video to YouTube. It's a great way to encourage your favorite video creators and to track what they're doing. It also connects you to the community and increases the chances that you'll find subscribers when you're ready to start posting videos and generating income or some exposure.

Finally, YouTube offers you the opportunity to embed videos right on your Web site or blog. In that same information box that features the Subscribe button is the computer code unique to that video. Simply click on it to highlight it, right-click to copy the code, and then paste it into your Web site or blog. The video should appear when you refresh the page. Video producers may select the option of not allowing their videos to be embedded, but you'll find most videos can be embedded. If you're interested in view counts (and you will be, as someone trying to monetize their videos), note that every time a YouTube video is watched, even on another Web site, it counts as a view. So when someone watches an embedded video, that counts as a view, too.

A LITTLE YouTube HISTORY

The history of YouTube is a compelling story. The Web site was founded in February 2005 as a video hosting site by former PayPal employees Chad Hurley, Steve Chen, and Jawed Karim. The company was officially launched in December of that year after it received venture capital from Sequoia Capital, of Menlo Park, California. Google acquired it for $1.65 billion in stock just about a year later, in November 2006. Today, YouTube operates as an independent subsidiary. The company is famously unprofitable, and as we write this, is feverishly developing ways to monetize all those eyeballs the site attracts. Deep pockets of Google aside, Wikipedia reports YouTube's bandwidth expenses exceed $1 million a day. No estimates of its revenues have come close to that outlay.

YouTube wasn't the first company to offer access to videos online, but its timing was excellent. In 2007, cofounder Steve Chen told *BusinessWeek* some of the key reasons for the company's success.

- The emergence of inexpensive video cameras

- The growth in fiber lines from 1999 to 2004

- The growth in the penetration of broadband access

In spite of that little problem of not adequately monetizing the site, YouTube's growth has been little short of miraculous. Today

YouTube spans the globe and operates not only in the United States but also in these countries and territories:

- Australia
- Brazil
- Canada
- France
- Germany
- Hong Kong
- Ireland
- Italy
- Japan
- Korea
- Mexico
- The Netherlands
- New Zealand
- Poland
- Russia
- Spain
- Taiwan
- The United Kingdom

In addition to English, you'll also find YouTube in the following languages:

- Chinese (traditional)
- Dutch
- French
- German
- Italian
- Japanese
- Korean
- Polish
- Portuguese
- Russian
- Spanish

As we write this, it's been fewer than four years since YouTube came into existence. That's quite an explosive level of growth for any company about as old as a preschooler! It's easy to understand, within this context, the enthusiasm we found whenever we spoke with someone who was gaining fame and some fortune through

YouTube videos. They have grabbed onto a rocket that's only just left the launchpad.

YouTube Myths

Every history comes complete with mythology, naturally, and YouTube's history is no exception. Here are some myths that surround YouTube, and we hope to dispel them now.

1. *All the good ideas have been taken.*
    That would be impossible, as brilliantly creative videos appear on the site all the time.

2. *You can't make money with YouTube.*
    Stick with us, and you'll meet people who do.

3. *Sophomoric videos are the most popular.*
    No, they're just the ones that get all the attention. Actually, according to the online video market research company TubeMogul, YouTube's most popular video category is Autos & Vehicles.

4. *Only teens and college kids use YouTube.*
    Yes, the under-30 market is well represented, but so are even younger and also older demographic groups. People of all ages help videos go viral by e-mailing them to friends and relatives and posting them on Web sites.

5. *YouTube is just for fun.*
    That's like saying there's nothing "educational" on TV, the newspaper only contains the comics, and the Internet is only a vast wasteland of porn and perversity.

6. *YouTube celebrities, like all celebrities, are "different" from the rest of us.*

   Not at all, in fact, most are even more average than the majority of us are.

7. *YouTube is a video free-for-all with no order to the chaos.*

   If you opened a vast reference book and jumped in without using the table of contents or index, you'd have to be prepared to waste some time. There are many ways to find what you're looking for on YouTube without just aimlessly browsing (not that there's anything wrong with that).

8. *To make money on YouTube you have to show some creativity and be prepared to work hard.*

   Oops, that one's no myth. It's completely true!

USING YouTube FOR FUN AND PROFIT

You're ready to learn how to produce videos and use YouTube not just for fun but to make money as well. While much of that process will still be fun, we're not going to schmooze you into believing it will all be games, fame, and fortune. The people we spoke to who were finding success on YouTube *were* having fun, but they were also working hard. If you want to follow their lead, you'll find yourself in the same position. The good news is, you are just as likely to succeed as anyone else who has found success on YouTube. Right now, YouTube is "a level playing field," according to Steve Hall, advertising guru and publisher of the advertising industry blog AdRANTs. YouTube success can strike anywhere and doesn't favor one type of company over another. "It's not about clout or who has the bigger hammer," Steve adds.

Throughout this book, you'll be finding out about everything from how to create and title videos to how to attract people to your videos and *maybe* even make them go viral. But, as much as we plan to help you, we also promise to be completely honest with you about the ups and downs of life on YouTube. Jay Grandin, of Giant Ant Media and his partner Leah Nelson launched a video production business thanks to the success they garnered from their YouTube video *How to Shower: Women vs. Men*. As of this moment, that video has had more than five million views, and Jay and Leah have posted more than 60 other videos. They're also in the business of producing YouTube videos for other individuals and companies wanting to find YouTube success. "It's difficult when the client is looking for a 'viral video,'" Jay told us. "It just doesn't work that way." So, we're not about to tell you we can lead you to guaranteed success. What we can do is show you how many others have found success and how you can effectively add your videos to the YouTube community in the hopes of doing the same.

Creating Your Videos

Chapter 4 is devoted to the subject of producing and creating good videos. We've gathered great input from dozens of interviews with YouTube pioneers, and by the time you reach Chapter 5, you'll be leagues ahead of newcomers starting out on their own. If you feel intimidated by the task, we're here to tell you to take a deep breath and relax. Yes, many of the people we've spoken with came to YouTube with video production backgrounds, but most did not. You don't have to be a Hollywood producer to create a compelling YouTube video. As a matter of fact, many experts feel the "amateur" approach is actually more appealing to the YouTube audience than the fully polished and professional look. You'll have to decide for yourself which of these makes sense in your case, but whether you want to do it yourself or enlist a professional, you'll make that decision based on a solid background and knowledge about both approaches.

Video editing software has grown to be simpler and less expensive. Many fully functional programs are actually free. So, once you've captured your video images, you'll be able to edit the final product yourself. Don't be discouraged if you don't yet know how to do that. Instead, remember our homemakers-turned-YouTube-chefs. They didn't know anything about editing video when they first began either. But, that didn't stop them from figuring it out. You have the added advantage of the expertise they—and many others—have been willing to share with us. So, you are actually starting out near the front of the line.

Perhaps the easiest part of this whole process is uploading your videos to YouTube—the actual transfer of your video file to the site. That is true today, and will only be more so in the future. Today's video cameras are not only cheaper than they used to be, they are also easier to use and more likely to come equipped with seamless uploading capabilities. Uploading videos to YouTube has become so important that video camera manufacturers have to make the uploading process simple to stay competitive. Trust us, it's as easy as clicking a mouse. If you can send e-mail, you can upload a video to YouTube.

Marketing Your YouTube Video

So, how on earth are you going to get anyone to notice your little video once you put it on the site? Good question, but it's not one we're going to answer in Chapter 1. Chapter 5 is devoted to that subject, and there you'll learn all kinds of clever ways to help get your video noticed. For the purpose of this discussion, we want to set the stage by telling you that you have just a small window of opportunity to get your video noticed while it's new. You improve your chances by being an active member of the YouTube community when you first start producing and then uploading videos. So, between now and Chapter 5, spend time on the site, rate and comment on videos, subscribe to the channels from the producers you like, and share the videos you enjoy. By the time you're ready, you'll have your own presence on the site.

WHAT I KNOW NOW

So, what are some of the key "takeaways" from this chapter? (We'll provide this sort of wrap-up for each chapter.)

- YouTube isn't just a site for sharing videos. It's an entire online community.

- According to demographics, YouTube users are spread all across the United States and are evenly divided between the genders. And 73 percent of YouTube viewers say they don't mind the advertising that appears on the site because those ads keep the site free to its users.

- YouTube is simple to navigate; uploading videos is a snap.

- YouTube partnerships mean revenue-sharing opportunities.

- YouTube is now an international phenomenon with more than 200 million visitors arriving at the site every month.

- YouTube has achieved this incredible level of success in the fewer than four years since its founding.

JUST FOR FUN

YouTube success comes most often to those who work hard and think creatively. But, let's get real: YouTube is fun! It just plain is. So, we plan to end every chapter of this book with something fun for you to do or enjoy. Since this is the first chapter, we'll reward you with a list of some of our favorite YouTube videos. Some came to us through our research. Some came to us through our kids who fall within YouTube's prime demographics. Some are little known and some are YouTube phenomena. But, we hope you enjoy them all. Go onto the YouTube site and search for them as they appear in the list. We've listed them in no particular order. Enjoy!

- *A Bunny & 2 Cats Playing Cards*
- *Charlie the Unicorn*
- *Evolution of Dance*
- *Flea Market Montgomery–Long Version*
- *Il Divo–Somewhere*
- *In The Motherhood*
- *Lynyrd Skynyrd Free Bird*
- *Obama Girl—I Got a Crush...On Obama*
- *Parkour*
- *Super Mario*

MARKETING YOURSELF THROUGH YouTube

Many of the YouTube successes who shared their stories with us were people looking for a new way to pursue a passion, expand an existing small business, or build a following that could translate into jobs and opportunities in the offline world. We also spoke with experts who encourage job hunters to post their résumés on YouTube to attract prospective employers, and even high school students who felt that their YouTube videos were the jolt that pushed their college applications from the rejection pile to the acceptance pile. Their stories, goals, and efforts may vary, but all told they prove that YouTube is not just a place to be entertained but also a tremendous tool that's available to all who choose to learn to use it. But first, who are these people who have paved the way for the rest of us?

They include performers, artists, businesspeople, barbers, writers, and even accidental celebrities. This last group once may have set out just to have fun, but now some have business managers and advertising agencies representing them and their financial interests! Which brings us to the story we promised you in Chapter 1: the story about Fred.

Meet Fred

Fred, otherwise known in real life as Lucas Cruikshank, is YouTube's number 3 most popular channel *of all time* as we write this. Lucas, shown in Figure 2-1, just for the fun of it

FIGURE 2-1: LUCAS CRUIKSHANK, IS MUCH MORE
WIDELY KNOWN AS FRED.

created the character of Fred, a six-year-old with hyperactivity issues, a chipmunk voice, and more family problems than 10 soap operas combined. He worked from his family's Nebraska farm with two of his cousins creating zany, zippy, crazed videos about the adventures of poor little Fred. His channel became so popular that today Lucas has an advertising firm that's hired him, Woo Agency, and a business manager, Jamie Dolin, and a future he probably never imagined would be his own. Oh, did we mention yet that Lucas is 14?

When Lucas and his cousins started uploading videos to YouTube, it was just a lark. But, Fred became so popular with the 9- to-14-year-old crowd, that he soon began drawing attention of another sort. The business professionals who help manage Lucas's future have leveraged his YouTube success wisely, and Lucas is now a spokesperson for Zipit Wireless, the makers of a handheld device for texting and sending instant messages (IMs). Zipit Wireless created the gadget for the preadolescent and adolescent market. If you are a parent of anyone from the age of about 9 through 21 (college age), you know just exactly how important instant messaging and texting is to this group. You probably also have felt the frustration of trying to get to the family computer to check your e-mail or having to be resuscitated after opening your cell phone bill to see the effects of texting overages. Enter Zipit Wireless. For a flat price of about $150 you can give that child a Zipit with nearly *unlimited* texting and instant messaging for a year.

When the Zipit people were ready to launch their product they turned to the Woo Agency to create a marketing plan. "We are a start-up, and nobody knows who we are," they told the agency. "We want to get into Target and Best Buy." Ralph Lagnado and David Abehsera of the Woo Agency gathered a group of young people from different parts of the country to see what they were on to that the adults weren't catching. It turns out that meant Fred.

With Fred on board, Zipit was featured in a new Fred video as his perfect solution to the problem of having a huge family and only one computer. Fred totally convinces his audience how cool and fun his new Zipit is as he disappears into the family bathroom to snuggle up in the empty tub and text message his little fingers to the bone. His running commentary expresses both frustration over his nutty family and delight with his new toy. It's an ad that doesn't even remotely seem like an ad, except that both Target and Best Buy almost immediately began selling the Zipit, and the company saw a *1,000 percent increase* in sales. That turned out to be a sweet return for the money Zipit spent getting Fred on board. "That's correct," Ralph told us. "It's a 'five-figures' deal, not on the lower end."

As for Fred? Well, he's a cewebrity! We spoke with his business manager, Jamie Dolan, who happens to also be one of Lucas's biggest fans. "Lucas has made this all happen on his own," said Jamie. Recently Jamie traveled with Lucas and his mom for a few days of filming in Mexico. "People mobbed him," Jamie said. "I've been in Los Angeles for 13 years, and I've never seen someone like that with no attention before, yet the kids all recognize him." We can attest to Fred's appeal to the younger generation. In a recent chat with a friend, we mentioned this book and Fred. "His name is Lucas," piped up her 10-year-old daughter, with the proprietary indignity only a kid can show when her own discovery is suddenly threatened by the grown-ups.

As for Lucas? He's working on season two of the Fred saga and living life with his fully functional, happy, and large family on their Nebraska farm. Future aspirations are still being discussed. "He, his parents, and I have talked about it," Jamie told us. "You want your family to have enough money so they can do something, but not enough so they can do nothing." Not the typical quandary most families with 14-year-olds face as a result of their youngster's drive and talent. Lucas' story illustrates two things: how almost anyone can become a YouTube celebrity, and how companies can use YouTube to reach a very specific market.

Well, the happy accident that allowed Lucas to strike it big as Fred isn't the type of thing any one of us can plan on. Most likely, you'll find YouTube success through the more traditional path of creativity mixed with hard work. We're going to assume you'll be more like the women behind *ShowMeTheCurry!* and that's just fine. They are certainly doing well and achieving their goals. Starting with a happy accident is fun, but now let's look at different types of individuals and how they've found ways to make successful lives through YouTube, but without that serendipitous lightning bolt.

PERFORMERS

For most of the history of humanity, there were dreamers who longed to become entertainers, but few ever achieved that dream. Of those who *were* able to realize that dream only a subset were successful enough to strike it big and live comfortably from it. The old stereotype of the stand-up comedian by night who drives a cab by day survives, because it's so true. YouTube has changed that in a big way. We met countless comedians who, although they may not be in the running for a star on Hollywood's Walk of Fame, were managing to pay the bills and rear their kids with money they earned from their YouTube celebrity. In addition to achieving their financial goals through product placements and YouTube partnerships, many of these performers could approach prospective auditions and job opportunities with living proof of their appeal to audiences. Let's look at the work of several of these successful entertainers to see what they have to teach.

Identify Your Strengths

"I think the thing is to do something you really like," advised Michael Buckley of *What the Buck?!* fame. "Create videos you'd like." Because YouTube offers a performer a virtually limitless audience, it's possible to create your own niche and then set about attracting like-minded people. When dealing with traditional media such as book publishing or TV broadcasting, you must demonstrate that your work has a broad enough appeal to make the decision makers who sign the checks believe that you can deliver. It can take years for a writer or broadcaster to get established. But, the cost of creating, posting, and distributing your own work is so negligible on YouTube that you can afford to put yourself out there and try different things to see what will bring you the results you're looking for. Asa Thibodaux is just one example of a comedian who made this work.

Meet Asa the Comic

Just before Hurricane Katrina struck New Orleans, native son and filmmaker Asa Thibodaux decided to leave. Newly engaged and concerned for his family's safety, he moved to Minneapolis and tried to set up shop. Back home in Louisiana, he'd done quite well making commercials for gyms, Cajun seafood places, gift shops, and nail salons. He'd always

FIGURE 2-2: ASA THIBODAUX IS ASATHECOMIC ON YouTube.

thought of himself as a filmmaker, but the commercial work put bread on the table. "I wrote the commercials," he told us. "The owners were pretty clueless, so they left the creative side to me. I'd create the commercial and then tweak it with the owners." Asa had every intention of continuing his business once he got up north.

Once he arrived in uncharted territory, however, he found his creativity wasn't enough. He needed connections. Where he once had a whole stack of reliable clients and associates in Louisiana, in Minnesota he was just a guy with no college degree and only his creativity to provide him with an income. "I'm used to working hard to provide for my family," Asa told us. "Businesses were looking at me like I'm crazy! I offered them commercials for $200 instead of $1,200, but they still wouldn't give me a chance." Lucky for the rest of us, Asa's fiancé kept encouraging him to try YouTube.

Less than a year later, when we spoke, Asa was a YouTube partner, with more than 100 videos posted, tens of thousands of subscribers, and hundreds of thousands of views. Yep, he was already a YouTube success. "My key ingredient," he told us "is to get people to watch by being real and relatable. You have to have a level of connectivity with people." To that end, he draws a lot of his material from his family life. One of his videos is entitled *Li'l Asa vs. Big Asa.* It would ring true to anyone who has ever tried to care for a toddler, let alone be the parent solely responsible for his care. Asa also touches on political and social issues, but always in a way that allows his viewers to be "in" on the joke. And, he stays sensitive to the needs and desires of his audience. For example, "I have to watch CNN less," he confessed to us, "because I could go on and on over that." Although he might feel better after this venting, he recognizes that it may not be what his audience wants to see every time he posts a new video. He brings his own sensibility and attitude to his work, but he does it with warmth and humor that allows everyone to feel connected.

Post Videos Consistently

Asa posts new videos every week. It's what he needs to do to be successful. This is a lesson for anyone who is trying to build an audience on YouTube. You'll need to post videos frequently and regularly if your goal is to build an audience who is interested in the type of entertainment you offer. "You can't post one video and then give up," Michael Buckley told us. "I probably had 100 videos before I got real exposure." Hetal Jannu and Anuja Balasubramanian of *ShowMeTheCurry!* echoed this advice for their cooking show, and it seemed a common thread among all the successful YouTubers with whom we spoke. Remember, if your goal is to attract a following, you'll have to give people plenty to follow. Paul "Fitzy" Fitzgerald, comedian, film critic, and sports enthusiast calls this "appointment TV."

Meet Fitzy

Paul Fitzgerald is a Boston native who attended the Tisch School of the Arts at New York University. He claims that he's not a film critic, just a big film nerd who studied film as an undergraduate. Still, he had been working the improvisation and stand-up circuit in New York for many years and earning a living doing voice-overs and such. When a close friend encouraged him to explore YouTube, everything began to change. Working together they started to post some of his routines on the site. "For the first three months on YouTube

FIGURE 2-3: PAUL "FITZY" FITZGERALD HAS FOUND FAME AND SOME FORTUNE WITH HIS CHARACTER ON YouTube.

we were getting just a few views. Whenever I switched over to sports, our views went up," he told us. In fact, his videos started spreading all over the Web. "We went from a couple hundred views to 25,000 views," Paul said. And so he found his niche. But, his own personal niche is more specific than sports in general. He focuses on Boston teams. "I've tapped into a fan base," he told us. "I've gotten some facial recognition in Boston."

Paul has some advice for others who want to follow his lead. First of all, as he cleverly puts it, to find success on YouTube you have to be a "Swiss Army knife." "You are your own creative, marketing, and advertising departments," he reminded us. He also offered these four rules to live by:

1. *With your work, tell the truth.* Everything I say as Fitzy is real. It doesn't sound as authentic if I say it myself. Put the truth in your performance. [This need for absolute sincerity and transparency applies to companies, as well, as you'll see in Chapter 3.]

2. *Be as regular as you can with your postings.* If you say you will have a new one every Friday, then do it. You'll hear about it if you don't post regularly.

3. *Be available.* If people start commenting on your videos or sending you e-mail, send them a comment back. Hit them back on their MySpace or Facebook pages. It means a lot to people. Fitzy reminds you, "Don't go big-time on me."

4. *If you're going to do comedy, be more funny!*

Paul is a YouTube partner, but his presence on YouTube has brought him even more exposure. "I get recognized when I go on auditions," he told us. He's also begun hosting an

Internet sports show for CBSsports.com. His efforts have given him a comfortable niche, and he's earning real money. "Thanks to Fitzy," Paul said, "my wife and I actually own our own apartment in New York."

PEOPLE IN BUSINESS FOR THEMSELVES

We'll grant that most of our readers aren't going to be performers or comedians. But YouTube isn't just an outlet for those blessed with prodigious talents. And even if you are a talented performer, you still have to think like a businessperson if you want to earn money with YouTube.

We're happy to report that plenty of businesspeople have turned to YouTube to grow their businesses and assets. In Chapter 3, you'll meet representatives of companies who are using YouTube in interesting and innovative ways, but here we'll focus on individuals, such as performers and professionals who are pursuing their business goals on the site.

Take the case of Dr. Steven Yarinsky, a plastic surgeon, shown in Figure 2-4, from Saratoga Springs, New York. Dr. Yarinsky's video is on YouTube's ShopDocVideo channel. He uses YouTube as part of his marketing efforts to attract new clients. "I post our video for prospective patients who then e-mail me for information about procedures," he told us. "The reaction has been excellent," Dr. Yarinsky reported. "The endorsement makes patients feel more comfortable calling for an appointment. Patients have told me that they saw it," he added. "We had over 600 views in the first two and a half months the video was up on YouTube." Dr. Yarinsky offered this advice for other physicians who are interested in using YouTube. "Use the video as a marketing tool to get patient leads into the office. Don't try to sell procedures—sell the doctor

FIGURE 2-4: DR. STEVEN YARINSKY USES YouTube TO HELP
MARKET HIS PRACTICE AS A PLASTIC SURGEON.

and the concept of calling and scheduling a consultation to meet
with the professional and to evaluate your needs." This advice applies to other professionals, of course, not just to doctors. An ac-
countant or lawyer wouldn't post a video of herself crunching
numbers or reading through briefs. Instead she should *sell herself*
and provide viewers with a means to get in touch with her to follow up.

Know Your Goals

Before you set out to create your business video for YouTube, be
sure you clearly understand the goals you hope to achieve. How can
you possibly address your audience before you fully understand
what it is you hope to accomplish? You also need to think about
what it is you want your customers to do after they have viewed
your video. Do you want them to follow a link to a Web site? Do you

want them to buy something? Like Dr. Yarinsky, do you want them to call? Do you want them simply to remember you and help you advertise your business by e-mailing your video to their friends? The end result you're aiming for will make a huge difference in the video you present. (New YouTube tools that allow you to add annotations to your videos, for example, can help make your video an even more effective marketing tool for you. We'll discuss these things in detail in Chapters 4 and 5.)

"I already had a marketing plan before I launched," said Arnel Ricafranca of Fitness VIP. Arnel, a fitness trainer by trade, is a Guru on YouTube. His Channel page appears in Figure 2-5. As we write this, he has more than 20,000 subscribers with a quarter million views. In addition to his YouTube presence, Arnel has some free Web sites and a membership-based site where he sells fitness items including benches and electronic books. Those sites have now had somewhere between 13 and 15 million views.

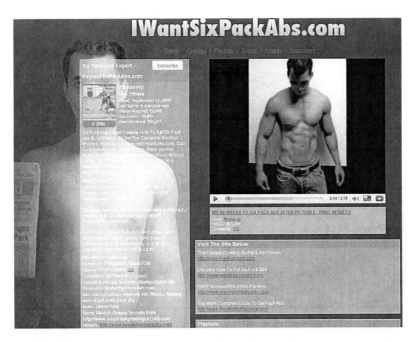

FIGURE 2-5: FITNESS TRAINER ARNEL RICAFRANCA USES YouTube TO HELP MARKET HIS FITNESS PRODUCTS.

"The more videos I have the more exposure I get," he explains. "So I keep adding them. Some do well and some don't, but I'm building keywords, like "six-pack abs" and "workout." I consistently upload one video a week. I don't give up, even when it's not going so well." Arnel's efforts have worked. When we searched Google for "six-pack abs" one of his videos appeared on the first page of search results. It helps that his YouTube videos all include the Web addresses for his most pertinent Web sites, and that the Web addresses for his sites are on every YouTube page that has anything to do with him. YouTube drives thousands and thousands of people to his Web sites. So Arnel is a shrewd YouTube businessperson, but he's also just a good businessperson all around. For example, Arnel knows his own business well enough to know how seasonality affects it. He recognizes that summer is a slow time for his industry. "In the spring I put up a lot, because people want to get into shape for nice weather," he noted. "Summer, I slow down, but I still keep uploading."

Advertise Around the Globe

Promoting your business on YouTube automatically makes your business part of a new global community. You'll be able to attract customers and clients from all those countries we mentioned in Chapter 1! If you plan to have a Web presence, YouTube must be a part of your strategy in the twenty-first century. It's just too vital a medium for you to ignore. And you can bet your competitors won't be ignoring it, even if you are.

Meet Davide Ricchetti

We "met" Davide on YouTube, and although he goes against our advice to post lots of videos, the one video he does have has dramatically changed his life. This 28-year-old artist,

FIGURE 2-6: DAVIDE RICCHETTI CREATES CUSTOM-
PAINTED GUITARS, SUCH AS THE ONE SHOWN HERE,
FOR CLIENTS ALL OVER THE WORLD.

painter, set designer, and teacher came onto YouTube at the
end of 2007. A year earlier he had begun to paint his own
musical instruments. Next he was custom-painting guitars
in his hometown in Italy. Today he paints instruments for
clients all over the world. You'll find him on YouTube at
RicDav79, but you'll also find his work through Goldhat3, a
singer/songwriter from Raleigh, North Carolina. The two
became friends through YouTube. Davide apologized for his
English when we corresponded, but we actually found him
so unassuming, "real," and enthusiastic that we'll share his

advice with you in his own words. He certainly writes in English way better than we could ever write in Italian! With very minor editorial changes, here's what Davide has to share.

1. *Please tell us about your business. For example, exactly what do you do, how do you get customers, and where do your customers come from?*

    I am an artist by profession, specifically a painter and set designer for theater. Since 2006, I started to paint musical instruments. . . . Then the people of my town . . . started to give me their instruments for painting. [At] the end of 2007 I created an account [on] YouTube, and I inserted a video with some of my creations. Now, thanks to this video, people contact me from all over the world to get information on my work. The important thing is to talk about your work with everyone.

2. *What are some of the more unusual things people have asked you to paint?*

    Ah! [They] often ask me to paint famous musicians like Jim Morrison, Jimi Hendrix, Simon and Garfunkel, Johnny Cash . . . but perhaps the strangest request was to paint the Crucifixion of Jesus.

3. *How do you use YouTube to promote your business?*

    The most important factors are creating friendships with each person; you can open new doors to new customers. To do this, [you] must leave messages on other channels, share videos, [and] rate videos of others, in short, building, day after day, . . . relations with other channels. You will sooner or later find people interested in your work.

4. *Have you gotten any business because of your YouTube videos? How do you know?*

Yes, through YouTube I created two guitars for customers in the U.S. and now [others are] being negotiated with customers [in] The Netherlands, Germany, and Spain. And all stem from [my] YouTube [video] . . . [and the efforts of] my client and new friend Goldhat3 [Mark Easley], [who] did . . . great advertising [for me].

5. *How important is YouTube to your advertising and promotional efforts?*

I think that YouTube is a [fantastic] channel of advertising . . . , better than a website, because on YouTube other people advertise to you sharing your movies or your channel. [It] is like a spider's web communication that magnifies increasingly . . . across the globe.

6. *Do you have any advice for people who would like to promote their businesses on YouTube?*

Create a beautiful account with photos [in the] background, a rich description of your work, videos, video favorites, [comments by and pictures of] friends, and comments of others. In short you must create a channel full of things and contacts. Sooner or later customers will arrive!

I hope to have been good.

It takes him anywhere between one to three weeks to complete a project depending on how complex it is. To watch the process, you can visit Goldhat3 on YouTube and search for "World Premier of the S&G Guitar." You won't be disappointed, and yes, Davide, we all think you have been good!

YouTube TEACHERS

One of the most popular YouTube videos is the type that teaches you how to do something. Whether you're looking for guitar lessons, improved gas mileage, or lessons in giving a good haircut, you're bound to find what you want on the site. We met Steve the Austrian Barber on YouTube and learned that he uses YouTube to promote his eBay business. He posts demonstration videos for different men's haircuts on YouTube and sells on eBay the DVDs and clippers do-it-yourselfers would need to actually cut hair at home. "I sold in pre-YouTube time, too," Steve told us, "but now it's easier and I get more page impressions than before, and sometimes more money." You'll find an example of Steve's work by searching YouTube for his channel *ausbar*. When we checked, he had nearly 100,000 channel views.

Perhaps our very favorite YouTube teacher is Kip Kedersha, known on the site as Kipkay. Kip, shown in Figure 2-7, has filled his channel with how-to videos that include such intriguing

FIGURE 2-7: KIP KEDERSHA, KNOWN ON YouTube AS KIPKAY, HAS TURNED HIS CREATIVE DO-IT-YOURSELF PROJECTS INTO A UNIQUE YouTube-FUELED BUSINESS.

subjects as how to double your gas mileage, how to escape from a professional set of handcuffs, how to chill a can of soda or beer in under two minutes, and how to turn red traffic lights green. Kip has a long and illustrious history as a "tinkerer and do-it-your-selfer." Now he's finding success with his videos on YouTube as they generate advertising revenues and rack up the views. Kip was kind enough to allow us to share his top five favorite tips for video success.

Five Tips from Kip

1. *Know your market.* Who are you trying to appeal to? The easiest way to determine this is to look at what the most viewed or most popular videos are on the site to which you're uploading. That will give you a pretty good idea of who your target audience is and what kind of content they like. There's really a wide range of tastes out there, and you might be surprised at the diversity of genres that have quite a large audience.

2. *Create a great video.* This includes a good story, audio, lighting, and editing. On the Web, less really is more—you only have a few seconds to capture the audience's attention, so engage them right away and get to the point quickly. Production value is also important. Not everyone is a professional videographer, of course, but do the best you can. Research different video techniques. Try to learn as much as you can about video production. Solicit feedback from your friends and family—it's always useful to see your work through the eyes of a first-time viewer (especially after you've been engrossed in a project for a

while). And practice—you really will see marked improvement in pretty short order.

3. *Make a good first impression.* When viewers are surfing a video site, they make decisions about what to watch based on a video's description and thumbnail image. Both of these can make or break the success of your video. In order for people to click on it, there has to be something that draws their attention—and you'll only be successful if that first impression is an accurate representation of what they're going to get once they start watching. A description that quickly tells the general story in the least amount of words is best. Think of it as a headline to your video. If you have the opportunity to select a thumbnail for your video, choose one that best represents the video and would attract a potential viewer.

4. *Be accessible, and communicate regularly.* If you have your own Web site, include the address in your videos or their descriptions. Lots of video sites have embeddable players that can drive cross-promotional traffic from your site to theirs—and vice versa. Take advantage of this. Also, provide an e-mail address on your site or in your videos—making it easy for the people who like your work to get in touch with you helps put a human face on it. This, in turn, can help drive viral distribution of your video, because people have a connection to the creator. As you establish connections with people, start building an e-mail distribution list that you can contact when you have new work to share. Some sites will do this heavy lifting for you through their "User Channels" functionality. This is a great way to collect and showcase all your work in

one place. And you can even have people subscribe to your channel—with subscribers automatically getting e-mail updates when you upload a new video. If the site you submit to allows people to comment on your videos, be an active participant—answer questions directly, and don't take criticism too personally. And be sure to comment on the videos you like—the world of online video really is about community, so be a good online neighbor.

5. *Put the power of the Internet to work.* There are hundreds, if not thousands, of Web sites and blogs dedicated to virtually every subject—and subsubject—you can think of. Become familiar with those that focus on topics for which your videos are well suited. Many of the people behind these sites and blogs are always on the lookout for content that will prove interesting to their readers. When you have a video that fits the bill, let them know about it! Just send a note or use the "Tip the Editor" function. If the site you submit to accepts embedded views, these sites can help generate views without any effort on your part. This is putting the power of the Internet to work for you!

VIDEO RÉSUMÉS: GOOD IDEA OR BAD?

By now you know we're big fans of video in general and YouTube more specifically. So naturally it seemed to us, at first glance, like a fabulous idea to promote yourself throughout the course of your next job search right on YouTube. You can put on your best suit, polish up your best presentation skills, and let prospective employees see firsthand how well you communicate. It wasn't until we actually talked to some professional human resources (HR) people and hiring managers that we realized it wasn't that simple. As it turns out, video résumés can be loaded with trouble and actually work against you in your job search. Most HR people dislike them. Let's look at this downside first.

Time Constraints

Many recruiters said they only have about 10 seconds to review a résumé, which is a bit humbling considering how long it can take to put one together. So, they don't have time to watch a video. Alison Mitchell, a longtime HR professional, estimates it would take her 60 to 180 seconds to assess a video résumé. Why would a busy professional take that time with your video when for the same amount of time 6 to 18 résumés could be screened?

Additionally, video can't be searched by keyword, which is how most employers first zero in on prospective applicants. You may very well never get your information in front of the hiring party if it can't be placed in a database and keyword searched.

Potential Legal Troubles

Judging prospective employees by the way they look can actually lead to charges of discrimination. Even if you don't intend to rule people out, a video allows you to get distracted by things like hair and clothing styles. "I've been the recipient of video résumés, and I have to tell you, they don't work," remarks Jasmine Pillay, owner of AfriZulu Consulting. "You end up looking at and assessing all the wrong qualities, no matter how seasoned or experienced you are." Jasmine went on to explain that "you actually end up remembering things that are irrelevant or that may actually sway your opinion negatively about the applicant, such as the colors of her clothing as it appears in the video."

Alison Mitchell agrees: "The most significant disadvantage to using video résumés is one that carries potential legal ramifications—the possibility of opening a door to discrimination in hiring." That can lead to a complaint with the Equal Employment Opportunity Commission. "You can't prove that you are not biased if you know the person's race or gender within seconds of viewing their image," she adds. To be especially careful, Alison notes that many hiring managers even reject photographs that accompany résumés.

Oops! The Wrong Impression

Unless you are experienced and very comfortable in front of the camera, it can be difficult to appear natural and make the impression you were hoping for. When you're creating videos for YouTube, you'll have your subject to focus on and you'll be busy getting your message across, but selling just yourself is a whole different thing. With the way video can be spread virally across the Internet, not only can a bad performance work against your current job search, but it can also haunt you well into the future. Executive search consultant Matthew Huffman confided that "there was a video résumé floating around Wall Street last year that was so incredibly bad it was distributed everywhere as a joke. I'm doubting that guy has a job even now."

On the Other Hand . . .

Now that you're well aware of the potential pitfalls, you're ready to look at some instances where video may prove to be a real asset to your job search. For anyone applying for jobs where "personal chemistry" is a key to success, as in sales, video can give you the edge you need to put yourself at the front of the pack. "If the candidate in question is applying for a sales role, then their ability to influence using their auditory and visual convincing skills is a totally fair way of assessing, and it provides increased value to both the employer and the candidate," said Matt Mills, business development executive with 1st Place. Or, in jobs where creativity and poise are important, you may be called upon to display the kind of skills that are best displayed visually. For actors, comedians, broadcast journalists, public relations specialists, and such, you may actually *need* a video as part of your application. Plus, the people who hire in those fields may be far more comfortable with reviewing candidates via video.

Dave Bricker, graphic designer, Web developer, and a marketing consultant on the faculty at Miami International University of Art and Design, related this story to us.

> I just spent a session reviewing agency portfolio sites with a group of college design, advertising, animation and visual effects (VFX) students. We decided that the two primary hiring criteria were "does the candidate have the needed skills?" and "is the candidate someone we'd like to work with?"
>
> Nobody reads more than 1 percent of any of the text on any of the Web sites. However, one site had a few short videos informally introducing the three company principals. There was light humor, and no attempts were made to be slick with the production values. Everyone agreed this was an excellent way to get to know the company beyond what their work reflected about their capabilities. The off-the-cuff quality of the presentation was very humanizing, and the general feeling was that it was comforting to have a better picture of who might be answering the phone and what sort of response you might get from them. We also felt it helped to discourage calls from people who would be more comfortable with a more "square-cornered" kind of agency, and that there was value in discouraging clients who weren't a good fit.

Aside from being useful when applying for jobs in visually creative, personality-driven, or performance-based industries, video may be a good asset if you're applying for a job where distance between you and the employer is a factor. When the degree of separation is from one coast to the other or even across international borders, a well-produced video may be the boost you'll need to compete long distance.

If You Decide to Do It, Do It Right

That phrase "well-produced" is the key element here. There are many video résumés on YouTube, and like any other video category, some succeed and most don't. If you do decide to produce a video résumé, make sure you do it well. You definitely wouldn't want to be the next Wall Street joke. Fortunately, Dave Bricker shared with us the following rules to guide you:

1. Keep the video short, light, and free from too many details that can be read once the employer is interested in the printed résumé.

2. Don't overproduce it unless you're trying out for a video production job.

3. Use Flash video, because everyone already has the plug-in, and the compression and quality are fantastic. (Adobe Flash player is available free of charge at www.adobe.com. Simply click on the "Get Adobe Flash player" button to download.)

Finally, if you do decide you want to represent yourself with a video, make viewing it an option on your standard paper résumé. You can do that by providing a link that will take the reviewer to the video on either YouTube or your own Web site. That way you give the hiring manager or recruiter a choice, and viewing it will be a conscious decision. The résumé you've provided ensures that all the data the company needs exists in simple, standard, searchable form, and you can use the video to convey how you might fit in with the organization. Advised Dave Bricker: "As a friendly, professional introduction, a video can give you a tremendous edge over the dozens of faceless résumés that offer a lot of factoids but which usually fail to answer the question that employers are asking subconsciously—do I want this person in my daily life?" Finally, although it may be more fun to create a video than a résumé, if you do decide to create a video you will still need that traditional résumé. Your résumé should be letter perfect before you turn your attention to the well-produced video representation. Then you can go on to sell yourself with both.

COLLEGE ADMISSIONS VIDEOS

The scene: Harvard Law School admissions officers are harrumphing around a conference table, studying materials from the latest batch of eager applicants. Open for discussion now: a fashion marketing major from a California public college. Fashion marketing? Well her LSATs were good, but then again, this was Harvard, and so were everyone else's. But their interest was piqued so they decided to look at the video part of her application. It wowed them! In it, the candidate speaks confidently and brightly about her commitment to the study of law. (Curiously, she also mentions she had been in a Ricky Martin video!) Of course, the fact the girl was Reese Witherspoon who also sometimes appeared in a sequined bikini, didn't hurt a thing.

Reese Witherspoon aside, the question is, should college and graduate school admission applications be bolstered with a video posted on YouTube? The answer? Sometimes. In some ways, the college admissions process hasn't changed at all over the last couple of decades. There is a very large pool of applicants all trying to get into the best schools. How schools are ranked is more salient than ever thanks to the heavily promoted US News and World Report yearly tally. If the young people you know aren't on top of these rankings (and they are), then surely their parents are. So, more and more applicants are vying for the same spots in the same highly rated schools.

With so many applicants, the review process necessarily often starts with statistics, which can be reviewed quickly and even electronically: test scores and grade point averages, for example. Subjective things count too, such as essays and recommendations, but for the more selective schools they are not usually evaluated until the applicant has passed the numbers test.

Suppose an applicant passes those all-important numbers hurdles. Often there are still many applicants who qualify, and selecting one over another depends on more subjective criteria. That's where those essays and recommendations come into play, as do extracurricular activities, and whether the applicant fills a gap in the school's freshman class. Admissions officers talk about building the class, not just filling the openings at the school. They are also encouraging online applications, with many accepting either what's known as the Universal College Application, or its older competitor, the Common Application. Completing only a single online application that's submitted to many schools saves students time, and makes it easier to apply to more schools. The rise in online applications is partly responsible for the greater number of applications that many schools are receiving. More applications mean more competition, so students need an edge to distinguish themselves, and video can be that edge. Once an application is online, of course, adding a video link to it is a snap.

According to Jannine C. Llonde, Assistant Dean of Admissions at the University of Virginia, certain categories of students are routinely providing videos as part of their applications. These include, as you might have guessed, applicants to visual or performing arts programs (traditionally art, dance, music, and theater). These are areas of study that have historically required auditions as part of the application process. Other students using them are seeking sports-related scholarships (often tennis, from our review of what's on YouTube), and nothing attests better to their wicked serves than a video. Czech Republic native Jakub Fejfar posted an impressive YouTube video showing his tennis prowess. But did the video make a difference? "I have to say that my video was received very positively," Jakub told us. "Not only did it help me find the school I was looking for, but also judging from the comments below my video it was received very well."

Fortunately, today's college applicants are also members of a generation that's quite comfortable with online video. Not only are many of these students adept at using sites such as YouTube, but they have also very often produced their own videos, too. Of course, a slick video won't replace good grades, test results, or recommendations, but it could give the student the competitive boost necessary to secure a spot in the incoming freshman class at his or her first-choice school.

WHAT I KNOW NOW

Here are some of the key takeaways from this chapter on how you can use YouTube to create or promote your own individual business:

- Lightning can strike, and anyone can become a cewebrity, but don't count on it.

- YouTube makes it much more likely for performers to support themselves and their families while pursuing their crafts.

- To succeed on YouTube, identify particular strengths and use them.

- Once you decide to market yourself through YouTube, post videos consistently.

- Use YouTube to advertise and promote work to a global audience.

- A video résumé may or may not be right for you; make a careful assessment before trying one.

- Inclusion of a video as part of a college application may be an excellent idea in certain circumstances.

JUST FOR FUN

And now, just because you deserve to have some fun on the site too, here are some more YouTube videos we've enjoyed:

- *Double Your Gas Mileage! 2X*

- *Fitzy Goes to the 2008 NFL Draft*

- *Fred on Father's Day*

- *Lil' Asa vs. Big Asa*

- *Killer Home Chest Workout with 10 Pushup Variations*

- *Pork and Beans*

- *Stink Bomb Revenge!*

- *What the Buck?!*

MARKETING YOUR COMPANY ON YouTube

et's pause for a moment to consider how adults take showers. It turns out, there's a big difference between the way men handle this ritual and the way women do. First women undress and carefully sort their laundry into the appropriate hampers. Then they use the shower as a chance to assess their figures. They may use a crushed apricot facial scrub, take a few moments to exfoliate with a loofah, and apply a variety of hair products. They gingerly step out of the shower onto a bath mat, and then oh-so-carefully wrap towels around their bodies and their hair. Next they're ready for the real beauty ritual to begin. Guys are all business. First off, they have much less to do in there. On the way in they admire their physiques. Once in there they wash a few key areas, play with the shampoo lather, perhaps urinate, and get the heck out of there. Bath mat? Do we have a bath mat? If his wife or girlfriend is around he may do a little dance to get her wet and have some fun.

Okay, this exaggerates things a bit. But almost all of us can find some truth in parody, and gender differences are captured in a hysterical YouTube video: *How to Shower: Women vs. Men.* The video was so funny and well edited that it helped launch a business for Jay Grandin and Leah Nelson, the cofounders of Giant Ant Media. Giant Ant Media's client list now includes large companies such as Steelcase. Jay and Leah are also producing a documentary film and Webseries in Tanzania and continuing to make online videos "just for fun." And as for the video that started it all? To date more than six million YouTubers have watched it (see Figure 3-1). There it stays on YouTube providing ongoing free publicity for Giant Ant Media.

So if even a shred of doubt remains that YouTube can change your life, just think of Jay and Leah. But, more likely than pursuing a life of video production, you'll want to use YouTube to further the aims of a company that already exists. That's fine and, we can help there too. With YouTube's rapid worldwide growth, it's no wonder that companies of every size, selling everything from soap to software, are successfully using the video-hosting site to advertise, raise product and brand awareness, and generate new income. In Chapter 2 we explained how individuals are using YouTube. Here we'll turn our attention to businesses and corporations that are exploring the opportunities available on the site. Some, like Giant Ant Media, have come into existence simply because the individuals behind them found success on YouTube and launched a whole new life from that success. And others are innovative technology companies with their roots planted in newly tilled soil and their eyes on the next new innovation. But, surprising as it may seem,

How to Shower: Women vs. Men

Rate: ★★★★⯪ 13,033 ratings   **Views: 5,805,305**

FIGURE 3-1: THIS SUCCESSFUL VIDEO LAUNCHED A NEW
COMPANY, GIANT ANT MEDIA, AND A WHOLE NEW LIFE FOR
THE TWO PEOPLE WHO CREATED IT.

some of them are older, far more established companies such as H&R Block and OfficeMax. You may have never thought of them as being on the cutting edge of a new endeavor, and yet that's just exactly where we found them.

There are YouTube success stories for virtually every type of business you can imagine. But finding success on the site is as much an art as it is a science. We'd love to be able to tell you that if you follow Steps 1, 2, and 3, your sales will soar, your boss will love you, and that big promotion will come next with the new cars and country club memberships. But, remember, we told you early on that we'd speak the truth to you, and so we're here to say you may or may not have the same type of success these companies have found. Chapter 4 will go into the specifics of creating great videos for YouTube from preplanning through uploading, and selecting titles and keywords, but this chapter will introduce you to companies that have used the site successfully. The goal is for you to reach Chapter 4 with your head swimming with potential. Your job will be to adapt the lessons these successful companies teach to your own specific corporate needs.

WHAT TYPES OF VIDEOS WORK BEST?

People who watch videos on YouTube are watching "video on demand." Although they may not mind the ads that accompany some videos, because they recognize them as being necessary for keeping the site free, they certainly don't want to feel as though they've clicked on a commercial. If they do, they'll click away as fast as their fingers will let them. If you're thinking about doing a video for your company, remember that it'll be best if it's entertainment first and advertising second. "So many people think you can just stick commercials on YouTube," says Bob Thacker, senior vice president of marketing and advertising for OfficeMax. "Video has to be more engaging and self-revealing," he explained.

You may think that the best way to find out how to get onto YouTube successfully is to spend countless hours wandering around the site to see what other companies are doing. Although it's always good to check out the competition, you may find that the great majority of your time is better spent thinking about your particular company, its product offerings, the customers you target, and the goals you're hoping to achieve with your videos. You are in the best position to understand the nature of your customer base and therefore the type of approach that would appeal to them most of all. Once you identify these specifics, you can turn your attention to creating appealing videos that will grab your particular audience.

Humor, Sex, and Parody

No, we're not talking about the last office party you attended. It's just that these three things tend to get the view counters jumping on YouTube. Amer Tadayon is chief executive officer of Render Films, a company devoted to creating digital video for the Web. When we asked him what works on YouTube, his answer was concise but informed: "It needs to be funny or shocking. Sex sells," he told us. Now, that doesn't mean we propose you create indecent videos for YouTube. The site wouldn't let those stay posted anyway, and we aren't that type of writer. What we mean is that you have to provide your viewers with some reward for watching your video, and these three things tend to reward the people who use YouTube. Amer told us about a campaign his company did for Brocade Software. The premise behind the campaign was a contest to dream of the best day off possible.

Through Wantyourlifeback.com Render launched a campaign to highlight the perfect day off for three different information technology (IT) workers forced to spend their weekends together catching up on work. Each shares a vision for the best day off possible. Viewers are invited to vote for the one they like best with the premise being that poor overworked IT staffer would then be granted the day off. For their European clients, the winner was a beautiful young woman. In a 30-second spot, you see her dressing for an evening out with a handsome young Italian man. They meet her husband in the driveway, and she calmly tells him in Russian, "Darling, I'll be home late." The two then get into a beautiful Porsche and drive away, leaving the hapless husband behind. It's clever, funny, a little sexy, and certainly shocking. Perhaps even more shocking though is that this campaign directly led to 200 qualified sales leads for Brocade. That's pretty amazing for a company that sells software for about $200,000 a pop!

Every industry and every company knows the things that most likely press a customer's buttons. We could easily come up with things that would parody the world of publishing, and you are likely able to spotlight the things that apply to your own customer base with the greatest relevance. Start there, and then think with a bit of a twist.

But, Don't Do This

It may be tempting, in the heat of a creative frenzy, to fabricate an event or persona in order to promote your product or company. Since you're thinking about creating entertainment-based video, why not just create some element of drama, post it as though it were real, and cleverly hide your corporate sponsorship? It's tempting, but it would definitely be a wrong step! In the world of online video, that's known as "astroturfing." You may not have yet heard of the term, but it describes a company's attempt to create a false grass roots campaign through the use of shills. The campaign then promotes the company's agenda. The problem with this is that YouTube viewers are pretty good at detecting fakes. Not only that, but if your video goes on to attract enough attention, your phony premise is bound to be revealed. Then, you'll lose all credibility on the site, and that is a situation from which it is very difficult to recover.

Some Famous YouTube Fakes

The first and still most famous YouTube deception was LonelyGirl15. You may remember, she was the star of a series of videos in which an attractive teen named Bree confided her travails and troubles to a video diary posted on YouTube. The quality of the videos, however, was a bit too slick. LonelyGirl15 was eventually found to be a 20-something actress named Jessica Rose.

In 2006, ABC news reported on a video spoof of Al Gore's Oscar-winning documentary *An Inconvenient Truth*. The video shows Mr. Gore as a most proper penguin addressing an audience full of bored penguins, and blaming global warming for all of our society's ills, including Lindsay Lohan's weight loss. When the *Wall Street Journal* went looking for the brilliant 29-year-old amateur filmmaker supposedly behind the video, they found a public relations firm instead. Evidently the firm DCI Group made the film at the behest of partisan interests, and although we're not pointing any fingers, one of the firm's clients is a major oil company.

Bride Has a Massive Hair Wig Out is another prime example. Three million people fell for the video showing a bride bursting into a hotel room packed with her celebratory bridesmaids. In an hysterical panic over the way the hairdresser did her hair for her big day, she throws herself into a frenzied fit that leads to her grabbing scissors and chopping into her hair in a crazed attempt to repair the damage. Although the ladies involved even appeared on interview shows as a result of the exposure, it soon came out that the whole thing was a hoax sponsored by Unilever in an attempt to promote its Sunsilk hair products.

Finally, if you've ever watched the MTV show *My Super Sweet 16* you'll understand the premise behind the series of videos highlighting an incredibly overindulged teenager known on YouTube as MacKenzie Heartsu. You'll see MacKenzie's happy and wealthy parents present her with a red Saab convertible for her birthday. Instead of being overwhelmed with gratitude, she launches into a tantrum, because what she really wanted was a blue Saab, and her parents should have known that! Subsequent videos show her trying to justify her lack of gratitude and her bad behavior, and finally she sells the red car on eBay for $9.99. Of course, by then she doesn't need it since Daddy went ahead and bought her the blue one she wanted. It's only in that last video, when she's turning over the keys to the lucky eBay shopper, that you see the whole thing was sponsored by Domino's Pizza.

In each of these cases, the truth behind the videos was revealed, and the resulting publicity was negative. Now, all of us have heard that any publicity is good publicity, but if you're trying to build brand loyalty and increase your company's exposure, you don't want to poison the well that holds your drinking water. These companies may have prevailed once, but they're unlikely to find a YouTube audience again. Remember what Fitzy taught us in Chapter 2: "with your work, tell the truth." It's good advice for companies as well as individuals.

Commercials created by and for large companies can find success on YouTube. *If they're creative and appealing enough,* the commercial itself can become a viral video. That's what has happened to a commercial spot for Sony's Bravia television. The spellbinding commercial features an array of clay bunnies that morph their way onto and through an urban cityscape. The resulting spot is so colorful and captivating that nearly 900,000 people have watched it so far. Sony wasn't behind the video on YouTube, however. It was actually uploaded by a fan of the commercial itself. Still, the fact is, whatever Sony spent to create that commercial, it spread much farther because of its appeal to the YouTube audience.

Instead, Think Webisodes

One very successful advertising campaign comes from a joint effort between Sprint and the Suave family of beauty products. This brand has long appealed to the busy but savvy shopper too smart to pay for higher-priced labels. They target the busy young mom most specifically—you know, the woman who has outgrown the need for flashy high-end beauty products and instead is looking for practical affordable products to help her look great. With this audience in mind, the companies launched a YouTube-based show called *In the Motherhood*. The show stars Jenny McCarthy and Chelsea Handler as two sisters both raising young children. Here's the conflict: Jenny plays the overly competent mom who has everything and knows just what to do with it; Chelsea plays the newly divorced mom who can't quite get her act together. To add to the fun, Jane Curtain makes occasional guest appearances as the overly critical mother of our stars.

Throughout the series, the sisters face the horrors of children throwing grocery store tantrums, the school bake sale, and of course, reminiscing about their own childhoods filled with sibling rivalry. Yes, the five- to seven-minute videos are product sponsored, but they are also so funny and engaging that they are well worth the brief commercial that begins and ends each episode. To make this whole idea even more fun, the folks at Unilever (the makers of Suave) took the series beyond YouTube. "Digital is far from done in isolation," Rob Master, North American media director for Unilever, told *Advertising Age* magazine. The company used *The Ellen DeGeneres Show* to drive people to the Web site InTheMother hood.com. There viewers could tell their own stories, and some of those were picked up for future episodes of the In The Motherhood show. This further connects viewers to the production and makes them more engaged than ever. Still, if your resources don't include this level of star power, don't despair. Other companies have found their own success with far more modest creations.

OfficeMax Does YouTube Right

When we spoke with Bob Thacker, the senior vice president of marketing and advertising for OfficeMax, we learned just how a big company can turn YouTube into an advertising

FIGURE 3-2: OFFICEMAX CREATED A SUCCESSFUL YouTube CAMPAIGN WITH PENNY PRANKS.

mecca. The folks at OfficeMax started with a very clear understanding of their strengths and weaknesses. They set out to make people feel differently about the company than the way they perceive OfficeMax competitors to be. "We realize it's a dull category," Bob told us. Sadly, we have to agree. Most of us don't get too jazzed about the next trip to the office supply place. With the idea that the best humor is real humor, Bob and his team set about creating the "Power to the Penny" campaign. Every one of the prank videos is real. They actually happened.

Just search YouTube for "Penny Prankster" and discover a series of hilarious bits, filmed with a camera attached to our prankster's messenger bag. Watch him as he tries to buy everything from a street vendor's hot dog to a car to an engagement ring with nothing but pennies. A chef at a fancy restaurant got mad, and so did a clerk at a convenience store—but a woman at a jeweler's was actually quite gracious. Of course, every video ends with the merchant declining the sale, and that's when OfficeMax's logo pops up with the phrase "We'll take your pennies!" and a sample product available for just $0.01 at your local OfficeMax store.

The *Penny Prankster* videos, created for a back-to-school campaign, have enjoyed millions of views, which is great news to a company with a back-to-school advertising budget that is one-seventh the budgets that their largest competitors have. "We have to be more creative," says Bob. Fortunately, Bob and his team have realized that "YouTube is the medium that our back-to-school audience is on. Not only kids, but moms, too," Bob explains. "Computers are our customers' companions."

As funny as the Penny Prankster is, and trust us it's hilarious, it actually was not the only successful online marketing campaign that OfficeMax was behind. For the Christmas seasons of 2006 and 2007, the company created an online campaign called Elf Yourself. Bob and his team created a Web site where you could go and add your face to an elf's body. Then you could watch as the little Elf-You danced to "Dashing through the Snow." For 2007, the company added multiple elves to one view, so you could elf yourself, your spouse, even the dog. The site was so popular that it had to be shut down for a time because of too much traffic. Oh, how tragic! Approximately 193 million people went to it, and it was the fifty-fifth most trafficked site during its time period. Even the anchors at ABC's *Good Morning America* show got into the act with their own little elf selves.

Bob and his team obviously know how to make YouTube work for their business. Both of these popular and successful campaigns cost a fraction of the price that TV advertising would require. Plus, the people who view them watch them by choice and freely share them with friends. The OfficeMax commercial *is* the show, so their advertising isn't subject to the "mute" button on the remote, and nobody scoots out to the bathroom or refrigerator until the "real" show starts again.

DO YouTube VIEWS EQUAL REVENUES?

By now you've seen some pretty impressive numbers. Lots of people view successful videos, but the question remains, does a high number of views translate into more revenue for companies? The scientific answer is, sometimes. Executives at Brocade Software were able to quantify the number of solid sales leads they turned up through their series of online videos. Other companies have been able to do the same. For example, Ogilvy & Mather, an international advertising firm, created the now famous *Dove Evolution* video. In less than two minutes the video shows, in time-lapsed fashion, all the work that goes into getting a premakeup model ready for a billboard photo shoot. More than eight million people have watched the video so far. "It was a great branding tool for the company," said James Dutton of Ogilvy & Mather. James told us that the video "resulted in $2.5 million in media value for a free upload." Ironically, the *Dove Evolution* parody, in which a handsome young man turns into a middle-aged slob, has also garnered 1.5 million views! As we'll discuss in Chapter 4, mimicry, if done right, works quite well on YouTube.

But, obviously, not every video campaign will achieve this type of success, and having an international advertising agency help isn't a bad thing either. Still, you don't have to go to the big guys to find success. We'll look at a few different examples, from people who don't have big budgets behind them, to get a better feel for YouTube's potential revenue boost, and we'll also share some experts' insights, too.

Good Business in a Real Estate Slump

In the summer of 2008, the real estate industry was suffering unprecedented challenges. The historic collapse of the mortgage industry, the glut of homes for sale, and the sinking economy made people very nervous about venturing into what is, for most Americans, the biggest investment of their lives. But when we talked to Fred Light, things looked quite a lot better. Fred is a real estate videographer who posts videos of homes for sale on YouTube. Fred was one of the few individuals doing very well in that depressed market. Based in New Hampshire, Fred noted that, honestly, the slow real estate market was a boon to his particular line of work. "Had the market been good, like a few years ago, this never would have happened," he told us. "By the time I got the video edited, the houses were sold." Fred said that part of his success was keyed not only to the poor real estate market, but also to the high cost of gas. "With the record number of properties on the market and gas prices what they are, people don't want to drive around all day long and look at properties. They can do it from home," he noted. As for the question about whether the video adds money to the sale, Fred told us that "video does a bunch of things, but people don't buy houses because they've seen the video."

"First they look at the specs, then photos, and then the videos," Fred explained. "By the time they watch the video, they're interested in the house. They already know a lot about the house." Fred further explained that video real estate benefits both the buyer and the seller. The buyers save time by thoroughly viewing the house before they physically arrive at the site. The seller benefits, because the buyers who do request a showing are actually interested in the property. It helps discourage the looky-loos who can make any seller crazy. And different properties can be presented through different focal points. For example, with a house in a great location the video can focus on the street and neighborhood. A very dedicated seller can appear on video and explain the enhancements made to the house during the time her family lived there. "The Realtor can appear," noted Fred. "It can be really helpful for branding themselves." Using these approaches, the house tour can feel far more personal than the usual trek through a stranger's house while soft music plays and the family is mysteriously missing. That's the way we've always house-hunted, but Fred's way sounds better. Increasing the number of prospective buyers, highlighting the services of an innovative Realtor, and easing the tension of a stressful market for both prospective buyers and sellers seems like a good thing for a depressed real estate market. And as for Fred, he earns a few hundred dollars for each video he produces, which has certainly helped him weather the real estate slump.

Let's Ask Some Experts

Although you have just seen a very specific example of how well-applied video can improve even a difficult business market, we can't make any broad statements based on such little data. The answer to whether or not video views boost sales numbers is a tricky one. We have a great deal of anecdotal information about how well companies are doing through their own YouTube exposure, but it's much harder to find the companies who will come forward and admit that their video campaigns didn't pan out for them. Before we proceed with more success stories, let's hear from a group of experts who have weighed in with opinions on the subject of high views equaling high revenues. To find these experts, we posted the question on the popular business social network LinkedIn. Here's what we learned:

- It could be great for building brand equity, but the audience you're reaching is the "gimmee" audience. They are looking for entertainment, and information to be beamed directly into their brains is small chunks—for free. After they've watched something on YouTube, it's another step to then go to a Web site, so they are already off to watch something else. If you have an awesome hook—more free stuff, for example—you might get some to click over. The person who comes up with the technology to embed a live link in a video could change that paradigm completely. (*Erica Friedman, Research Manager, Nielsen Buzzmetrics*)

- We have just started to use YouTube to promote our advertising video projects online. For us, it is just another venue for FREE online advertising. It will improve our link popularity on the Web and may generate some additional interest for our work. Now, will it generate real sales? It is too soon to tell, but it is part of our online marketing strategy! I'll be able to tell you more in a few months! (*Catherine Chevalier, Account Manager and Owner, Not Maurice*)

- YouTube is simply a free tool. It has great potential for advertisers and marketers to promote their products or services. We all know that if the video is done properly the user's next step is either to visit a major search engine or visit the homepage of the product/service. I would say though that with proper supervision, realistic goals, targeted messages, and targeting specific users (not the entire Web) you will hopefully turn some of that exposure to revenue. Research has shown that the more verticals the advertiser/marketer targets, the much higher and better the potential for return on investment can be. (*Enock Belomy, Interactive Marketing Executive*)

- There's nothing wrong with exposure, as long as the stuff is relevant, otherwise it's just noise (and it's too noisy anyway). (*Chris Von Selle, Managing Director, JWT*)

- Common sense tells you that any exposure is good exposure and that can lead to sales as long as you get people to YouTube in the first place. Directing traffic to the video requires some creative and not-so-creative marketing; however if the topic is HOT, people will find it via searching or viral word of mouth. Whatever you post, treat it like an ad and make sure the quality represents the product or at least is unique enough to create a buzz. (*Julie Gengo, Marketing Coordinator, HealthWalk*)

- If the YouTube video is reasonably well targeted and production values match expectations of the target, you'll increase both exposure (virally) and sales (call to action!). (*Greg Padley, Account Supervisor, New York–based RFC&P*)

- It is impossible to measure the amount of people who will watch a video now, and when it comes time to make a purchase, remember your brand above others. Even if the video does not turn into automatic direct sales, certainly it puts your brand ahead of another company, which did not use YouTube, in the mind of the video viewer. (*Sara Wells, Graduate Student, Murray State University*)

- Is it ever really a bad thing to have people see and hear about you and your business? (*Scott Welch, Sales and Marketing Professional*)

These expert opinions run the entire spectrum of whether or not YouTube exposure will lead to cold, hard cash. As mentioned previously, OfficeMax, Brocade Software, and Fred Light are not only doing well with their YouTube ventures but are also able to report solid earnings thanks to the site. With the voices of these experts echoing, it's time to look at a few more companies to see what success they have found and how. The experts have offered a good reminder of the warning issued early in this chapter. YouTube success *does* happen and *is* possible. It's just not that easy to quantify specific ways to make it happen (although we'll offer some specific ideas in Chapter 5 and 6). That's why the inspiration of others who have used it to enrich their companies can be so valuable.

Blendtec and the Story behind *Will It Blend?*

We spoke with George Wright, vice president of marketing for the Blendtec blender company. Blendtec is a well-established privately owned company known for making high-quality industrial blenders. According to the company's Web site, if you've had a smoothie, milkshake, or coffee drink prepared in a restaurant, you've most likely enjoyed the results of Blendtec's work. Founder and company owner Tom Dickson has been perfecting his blenders since the 1970s. When George Wright joined the company as vice president of marketing, the company was hoping to expand and bring brand awareness to the consumer line of blenders. Sure, professional chefs and restaurant owners knew all about the commercial side of the product line, but nothing much was happening for the home market.

FIGURE 3-3: TOM DICKSON OF BLENDTEC HAS BECOME
AN UNLIKELY YouTube STAR.

"We did all the basic branding things in line," George explained. "That's when I happened on the wood shavings." George is referring to the wood shavings on the floor of Tom's test lab. So it seems Tom has had a longstanding history of testing his blenders by trying to blend unusual objects. The wood shavings were from some two-by-four planks he'd been grinding. "Everyone else thought that was normal, but me. I saw an opportunity."

Why not take this quirky procedure for testing the company's blenders and turn it into an Internet phenomenon? This was a perfect blend (oops, pun intended) of advertising and video. With a budget of $50, George bought a lab coat for Tom and a Web address, willitblend.com. That's the microsite that supports the video series both on the site and on YouTube.

"I carved out a day with my video producer and Webmaster and took Tom into 'extreme blending.' He was just going to blend one thing at a time, 8 to 10 things total," George told us. "We tried to be as unscripted as possible. We tried to capture the reality of the event and were just as surprised at what will blend as the audience is." With filming wrapped, George sent everything off with his video producer who came back a few days later to say it was hilarious. "We had so much fun with it," George chuckled.

Some of Blendtec's videos have received millions of views. The company now has 75 videos on YouTube, and more than 100,000 subscribers. All the videos begin the same with an unassuming Tom asking the question, "Will it blend?" Next Tom is in the lab for a quick test, and viewers have the answer in fewer than two minutes. None of Blendtec's videos run longer than that, although today YouTube is stuffed with lots of other *Will It Blend?* knockoffs that do. In the past six months, Blendtec has seen an increase in views on their own microsite. That site exists just to highlight the quirky videos, but it also allows a simple click through to the Blendtec Web site, where viewers have the opportunity to shop for and buy the blenders. And as for sales? Have all the views turned into profits for this modest Utah-based maker of blenders? "We're a private company," explained George, "but we've seen 500 percent increases in our blender sales." That's a pretty respectable rate of return for an advertising campaign that began with a $50 investment!

George shares some insights into why this campaign has been so successful. "People have used social media for years to show things for a lot of reasons," he notes. "Very few companies have done the work to create amazing content to sell their products. That's why this campaign is so exciting. We used social media for business purposes. Advertising doesn't interrupt anything, because we're not creating advertising, we're creating content. We wanted to create something people would want to see."

HOW CAN YOUR COMPANY USE YouTube?

The answer to the question of how a company can effectively use YouTube will be as varied and specific as each company that's approaching the YouTube site. We hope by now you've guessed that your venture onto YouTube could bring your company anything or everything or nothing at all. Sure, serendipity might strike as it did for Blendtec, springing from a pile of wood shavings on the floor. Or, you may find yourself at the center of a

FIGURE 3-4: H&R BLOCK FOUND SUCCESS WITH ITS VIDEO CONTEST *ME AND MY SUPER SWEET REFUND*.

media frenzy like the Elf Yourself campaign. Still many other companies have offered up videos that went largely ignored. One company you may never have guessed would have found success in this emerging field is the old and reliable H&R Block. The tax preparation firm has had a very successful video campaign centered on a video contest entitled *Me and My Super Sweet Refund,* a piece of which is shown in Figure 3-4. We'll talk a lot more about YouTube video contests in general and this one specifically in Chapter 5, but the company's video adventure left its marketing staff with some solid advice to share. Paula Drum, vice president of digital tax marketing with H&R Block, boiled down this advice to three easy concepts:

1. *Understand the community—YouTube is about creative expression.* Don't try to just run your brand campaign. It will lead to negative backlash.

2. *Don't expect anything to go quite like you thought it would.* It is a live and dynamic community. If you are successful, there will be some surprises along the way. How you react to the surprises will also be a reflection of your brand.

3. *Be prepared to adapt and change as you go.* You can't be rigid. Launch, learn, iterate.

Beyond brand awareness and advertising buzz, companies can use YouTube in a number of other ways. We've spoken with representatives from technology companies to medical institutions, from political commentators to writers to small retail operations. It seems the reasons to turn to YouTube and the resulting experiences are as varied as American commerce.

Recruitment

More than 35 years ago Acadian Ambulance Service, Inc. started with two ambulances and a staff of eight employees. Today the company employs more than 2,500 people and their fleet of equipment includes medivac helicopters. They provide service all along the coast of the Gulf of Mexico, from Texas through Mississippi. The company prides itself on providing the same kind of emergency response to rural areas that was once reserved only for those who lived near major cities and their surrounding metropolitan areas. Acadian Ambulance uses YouTube to post videos the company has already created. Most of those videos end with a Web address so people interested in becoming emergency medical technicians (EMTs) or paramedics can click through and learn more. Has the campaign led to greater recruitment numbers? Acadian Ambulance has empirical proof. Says a company representative: "The increased interest in becoming a medic was measured in our survey we distributed during the last enrollment class. Many of the students had seen the videos on YouTube and made comments." Since the videos had already been created as part of the company's basic operations, this increased interest in joining the emergency medical responders cost the company nothing but the time it took for someone to upload and process the videos to the site.

The medical school at the University of Alberta had posted a few videos to YouTube before, but none caused quite the stir as Diagnosis Wenckebach. This video, shown in Figure 3-5, is a parody of Justin Timberlake's music video Sexy Back. Instead of the suave singer and dancer performing surrounded by sophisticated and beautiful people, Diagnosis Wenckebach takes place in a hospital setting, and the music video is performed by medical students and other staffers. "I know quite a few applicants to the University had heard of the video or seen it," Jon Hilner told us. Jon cowrote the script and is the lead singer, but he's very quick to point out that the

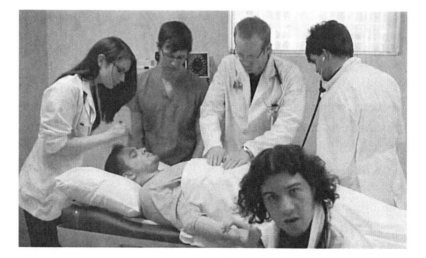

FIGURE 3-5: *DIAGNOSIS WENCKEBACH* BECAME A VERY SUCCESSFUL VENTURE FOR THE MEDICAL SCHOOL AT THE UNIVERSITY OF ALBERTA.

final project was a collaborative effort that everyone involved enjoyed creating. "I think what is more appealing than the video itself is the fact that it was made by medical students, and that it has had such support from the faculty," Jon told us. That sends a strong message to prospective students about the culture of this particular medical school. The appeal is quite obvious because, when we last checked, the video had more than 600,000 views. Now, those can't all be prospective medical students!

Education on YouTube

Aside from the promotional and recruitment value of the *Diagnosis Wenckebach* video, it also serves as a useful educational tool. Through the catchy tune and the repeated lyrics, students and newly diagnosed patients can learn about this particular heart arrhythmia. "It is such a subtle learning aid," Jon said, "and let's face it, it's totally nerdy. Justin Timberlake's song is about being the sexiest thing alive, but to some there's nothing sexier than being a big nerd!"

Acadian Ambulance also uses videos for educational purposes. The company has posted videos to teach techniques for assessing pediatric accident victims, safely lifting the injured, and calculating correct drug doses, to name just a few. So whether or not someone decides to work with this ambulance company, the Acadian Ambulance company has provided plenty of learning opportunities for EMTs and first responders all over the country and the world.

How-to videos are a very successful and popular niche on both YouTube and the Web at large. We saw in Chapter 2 how Kip Kedersha of Kipkay has built a whole business for himself through his online tinkering, but many companies have knowledge that could easily be shared in a video format. Think about what your products can do and how you could help educate the public in their use. There's a niche out there for just about anything you can think of teaching. According to the Pew American and Internet Life Project, seven million people search for some form of help online every day. Do they have a suggestion for companies looking to produce videos? Follow those searches!

Political Activism

Perhaps nothing has returned democracy to the hands of the people quite like the Internet. The generation now voting for the first time has never known a time when the Internet wasn't part of their lives. Campaigns raise money, build momentum, and stay in touch with supporters through social networking and Web sites. Why should social media be left out of the mix? When we spoke with Fred Light, he told us that an associate had asked him to cover the arrival in New Hampshire of one of the U.S. presidential candidates during the 2008 primary season. As the two men got to talking, Fred realized that he didn't know how this particular candidate felt about the issue at hand. His first thought was to hop onto YouTube, and sure enough within just a few keystrokes, he was watching a snippet of a speech this candidate had delivered on the subject. As quickly as that, he realized that he also had no clue about what the opposing candidate had to say on the subject. Once again, a few keystrokes later he had his answer playing right on his monitor in the form of another delivered speech.

"When speeches are posted on YouTube it's like adding seats to a room," said Arun Chaudhary, filmmaker and film professor. His team followed the Obama campaign and as of July 2008 had posted 1,500 video clips on YouTube. One video, Obama's speech about race in America, had received more than 4.6 million views.

WHAT I KNOW NOW

Here are some of the key takeaways from this chapter on how you can market your company effectively on YouTube:

- The path to YouTube success isn't clear and may not be direct.

- Humor, sex, and parody are popular on YouTube.

- Plan videos for the company that will be content driven rather than advertisement driven. Create something other people will want to see.

- Don't even think about doing a phony set-up. The perpetrator will be found out.

- A successful campaign on YouTube need not be expensive.

JUST FOR FUN

Here are some more YouTube videos we've enjoyed:

- Cat and Crow

- Chocolate Rain

- Eddie Izzard—Death Star Canteen

- In The Motherhood

- OK Go—Here It Goes Again

- Roadmasters

- Skateboarding Dog

- Sony Bravia Rabbits

CREATING YouTube VIDEOS

There's a director's chair on the set now, and your name blazes from the back of it. Here's the chapter we've been working toward. Undoubtedly, by this point you just can't wait to get that video camera out and get started. Everything you have learned so far should be swimming in your head along with images of the Dancing Man, Michael Buckley, Obama Girl, Will It Blend?, OfficeMax's Penny Prankster, and—who knows?—maybe even Fred's still in there! Now you know just how many individuals and companies have been successful on YouTube. And you want to be the next success story yourself. So, settle in for the last lesson you'll need before you are actually staking your claim in a corner of YouTube. You're going to get lots of great theories, facts, details, and advice about creating your own successful YouTube videos.

Please keep in mind that the subject of creating great videos has been covered in many excellent books. We could have included everything you'd need to know about the technicalities of videography here in this book, but then we would not have been able to tell you all about making money on YouTube, or share with you all the great insights from the people who have been making money on YouTube, or explain how to make it most likely that people will find your videos on the site once you've posted them, thereby leading toward earning you money. So, we are honestly stating right up front that video recording is not our area of expertise. We will, instead, share with you the wise counsel of the many successful video producers who spoke with us and were happy to share what they've learned along the way. We would not be offended if, by the end of this chapter, you feel we've stirred your appetite, but not filled your belly with all the information you'll need to become a video producer. Consider this chapter the appetizer. When you're done you can decide if you still want an entrée.

Let's start with a little practical philosophy. As with all creative processes, there are two essential parts to creating YouTube videos, and the one that is less fun comes first:

1. *Preplanning.* This is where you put on your thinking cap and let yourself dream. Just how do you envision your final video? What will it look like? Once you have your creative image in mind, you'll need to break the project into manageable steps, not only so you'll know what you need to do next, but also so that you can put all the equipment, sets, people, and props together before you begin.

2. *Creating the video.* Here's where you get to actually start filming and learning firsthand how to tell your own story through video. You can't rush into step two until you've thoroughly completed step one. You'll see the difference careful preplanning can make even to your first few video attempts. Although those first attempts may not become smash hits, you want to feel that you learn something useful with each video you make. Careful planning makes that more likely to be true. Don't forget that this part of the process also includes careful editing. Editing is what turns the filming into storytelling.

Not to rattle your confidence, but there's also a very important third step, and that's getting as many people to view the video as possible after you've created it. Don't worry about that important topic now, because it will be covered in Chapter 5.

HERE'S WHAT YOU'RE UP AGAINST

You will be competing for the attention of your audience with other YouTube video producers as well as with all the "noise" that accompanies life in the early part of the twenty-first century. We're not necessarily talking about the kind of background noise that Manhattanites endure each day or about that obnoxious neighbor who insists on dragging out the leaf blower at seven-thirty on a Saturday morning. Instead, we're referring to the many forms of media and so many associated messages competing for our attention every day, no matter where we live. All of us reside with a certain level of noise going on in our heads all the time; it's the modern-day battle for our mind space. Our friends at the AdRANTs advertising blog have compiled the following list of media that's swirling around us these days.

What's competing for your head space[*]:

- *Cable* TV and media
- *Consumer Created* content
- *Desktop* ads
- *Direct* advertising
- *Events*
- *Games*
- *Guerilla* marketing
- *Human* advertising
- *In-flight* media
- *Magazines*
- *Mobile/Wireless* communications
- *Newspaper*
- *Online* advertising
- *Outdoor* advertising
- *Packaging*
- *Podcasts*
- *Point of Purchase* displays
- *Posters*
- *Radio*
- *RSS* (rich site summary) feeds—delivery of regularly changing Web content
- *Social* networking
- *Specialty* advertising
- *Television*
- *Weblogs*
- *Yellow Pages*

All these are also your competition, and we didn't even include your wife, husband, partner, kids, pets, job, civic organizations, and chores. So now you see very clearly that there are some compelling reasons why you need to make your videos stand out. Most people have the attention spans of flies, and it's not entirely their own fault. It's just the way the situation has become as folks adapt to the bombardment of all this input. This attention span challenge is especially acute for younger people—the so-called digital natives—

---

*Words in italics are specific AdRANTs categories, for which they regularly provide up-to-date information on their Web site (www.adrants.com).

who have grown up with the Internet and hang out in numbers on YouTube. And remember, even once someone is on YouTube and watching that video of yours, millions of other videos are merely a click away.

PREPLANNING: RESEARCH AND GOALS, GOALS AND RESEARCH

Most people ultimately make money with their YouTube videos by grabbing a lot attention—a lot of views. Once you have a lot of views, many things can happen. YouTube partnership is just one of them. As you know, YouTube partners earn revenue from the ads YouTube places on the page showing its videos. You can also create a Web site or even a microsite where your viewers can land to take an action such as purchasing what you sell. That's called a "landing site." So, as you begin your planning, the first thing to ask yourself is, what do I want my viewers to do when they're finished watching my video? The answer to this question varies greatly depending on each video producer's goal. Let's review a couple of individual success stories now to see what the ultimate goals were in building YouTube success.

Goals Set and Achieved on YouTube

Arnel Ricafranca, fitness VIP, wants to build his Web presence as a fitness expert. He also wants to promote and sell his workout videos and his fitness equipment.

Hetal Jannu and Anuja Balasubramanian created *ShowMeTheCurry!* on YouTube to share their cooking expertise and garner a following. They hold the ultimate goal of earning money through sponsor product placements and advertising sales through their own Web site, where an entire community of Indian-food-loving folks come to gather.

Asa Thibodaux, Michael Buckley, and Paul "Fitzy" Fitzgerald are performers who have built robust followings through their YouTube efforts. That is bound to make a great impression at the next audition. It's also led to local TV shows, corporate sponsorship, and plenty of publicity.

Ben Relles, Jay Grandin, and Leah Nelson launched businesses with their YouTube videos. Ben's barelypolitical.com Web site was born with the *Obama Girl* video, and Jay and Leah find themselves operating a video production company after having a YouTube smash hit.

Acadian Ambulance and the University of Alberta never set out to strike it big on YouTube; rather, they intended to create an enticing recruitment piece that would bring them good candidates for new employees and new students.

Kip Kedersha found the perfect outlet for his unstoppable do-it-yourself energy. Now he's helping people increase gas mileage, turn red traffic lights green, and stay safe from the world's most dangerous battery.

So the reasons for going onto YouTube are varied, and your own reason may not have even made this list. But you have to know what you hope to achieve with your videos before you start to produce them. Even if that goal changes dramatically as you post videos and gain experience, at least decide the motivation behind your first video before you get started.

A Closer Look at What Works on YouTube

Up until now, a lot has been mentioned about the culture of YouTube and what seems to be popular on the site. But, how does that issue relate to what feels right for *you* and your own brand of video you plan to bring onto the site? If you followed the advice in Chapter 1, you know how people search for videos, share videos, and comment on them. You also can find channels of interest, and you've begun to make yourself part of the YouTube community. As part of your education, you no doubt have been viewing lots of videos, too. With that experience in hand, you by now should have a good idea of what works on the site. But since we're putting the pedal to the metal now, let's get even more specific. Here are some things that work well on YouTube:

MIMICRY

Videos that piggyback off of other successful videos have a grand history of success on YouTube. Search, for example, under "Chocolate Rain." You'll find the media event that started it all, Tay Zonday's moving and original song that now has 28 million views. But this search will also pull up more than 12,000 other videos! Some are parodies, or remixes, or covers. "Chocolate Rain" is incorporated into a McDonald's ad, someone sings the song in reverse, Darth Vader sings it, and Muppets move to it. Many of these videos received thousands of hits, some a million or more—all tallies way above the average for YouTube video. So by playing off of a hit, creators of those other videos found their own success. It was simple enough for us to find them by using "Chocolate Rain" as a search term, and that's most likely how many others found them too. The presence of these videos doesn't make the other YouTube video creators any less creative or more crass than those from any other medium. How many super-heroes made it to the big screen after *Superman*'s success? How many various types of souls were soothed by chicken soup after that first book came out? Business-minded people who create books, or motion pictures, or YouTube videos often go back to one great idea to find yet another way to get a hit from it. So don't be afraid to incorporate elements of other successful videos into your own. Just be sure you're bringing something of your own personality to it. Not all the pseudo- "Chocolate Rain" videos made it big. If your video isn't good, linking it to a big hit won't by itself lead you to success.

THE UNEXPECTED

It's a challenge to plan for this, but the fact is that the unexpected flat-out works on YouTube. When we spoke to an agency that was brainstorming ideas for a car client, they said they were planning to "just flip some cars upside down." This plan didn't strike us as odd at all—this is YouTube after all. Being weird isn't necessarily a bad approach, as you can't deny that many have been successful with it. Remember, and we can't overemphasize this: it's a market that has grown numb to conventional ads. "What I've seen YouTube celebrities do," Asa Thibodaux told us, "was to take something that people really cared about and make it their own. Make it something that other people could relate to. It's the 'weird' of that reality where the hit occurs." So remember, weird is wonderful.

HUMOR

Look at your average computer user. Okay, look at us. Hunched over, staring vapidly at a screen. Where are the yucks? They are on YouTube, which is why we feel humorous videos are so popular. They're a sharp and welcome diversion. It's no wonder that humorous videos are the ones that most often make the e-mail rounds. Who couldn't use a few more laughs?

TOPICAL COMMENTARIES

Michael Buckley has forged a career from his fresh-from-the-headlines rants on YouTube. That shouldn't surprise anyone. There's a long tradition of commentators mining headlines for material. Look at Lenny Bruce and Mort Sahl from the 1960s and Chris Rock and Bill Maher from the present day. Also consider Johnny Carson and David Letterman; the fact that Carson's and Letterman's monologues have been so topical is one reason why they fall so flat when they are rerun. Months or years later, the guests may still be interesting but the very topical commentary is as likely to elicit a "huh" as much as a "ha."

Sex

Do we really have to spell this out for you? This isn't news; it never is. Sex gets people's attention, even when it's tangentially related to a video. For example, Jay Grandin of Giant Ant admitted to us that one reason why the *How to Shower* video scored over five million views was that the thumbnail associated with it showed Leah washing her hair. He suspected some guys clicked through to watch it just on the chance they might catch a peak of her naked.

Be Clever

Many of the people who use YouTube are a tad nerdy (by definition they use computers for more than work). But they appreciate it when someone has gotten their attention by being clever. There are beat-boxing parrots, chipmunked celebrities, and political statements of every variety, even political statements about political statements. Bits and brains just go together.

Be Aware

Creating effective videos isn't a cut-and-dried process, which is one reason why you're holding this book in your hands. YouTube is a moving target, and a huge audience made up of many subaudiences. Crossover videos are still pretty rare. Remember that YouTube's audience is international in scope. Humor that only Americans would get may go against your goals. For example, Serena Software, which specializes in business software that encourages collaboration among far-flung employees (they actually call it "business mashups"), naturally saw YouTube as a good way to reach its market. Their first video was *Mashup in a Can*.

This was a playoff on the story of the congressman who got caught soliciting sex in a public stall at an airport restroom. *Mashup in a Can* received lots of views domestically, but not internationally, because many people overseas were not familiar with the scandal. Of course, what one person finds clever or humorous another finds vapid, so you always need to get input from other people. Brad, for example, thought a video featuring Tyra Banks in a rant done in a Darth Vader voice was hysterical, and he dared Deb not to laugh at it. She didn't, she didn't even have to struggle not to. It wasn't funny. Not even a little. Tyra was really upset, and it was sad to watch.

Research Hot YouTube Videos

YouTube always has Featured videos on its home page. These are videos selected by YouTube staff editors to be featured in YouTube's prime spot. You already know they're doing well. But when you click on the Video tab, you get to see a lot more videos currently being touted on the site (see Figure 4-1). Check out the Most Viewed and the Most Discussed videos to see what's currently getting passed around the YouTube community. Also take a look at Rising Videos. This is instant and free market research there for the clicking.

Review the YouTube Blog

The YouTube blog at www.youtube.com/blog may also give you some ideas for what YouTube itself is noticing and promoting. Many of the entries will be topical and just reflect what's in the news (for example, the GOP convention was a hot topic in September 2008). But there are also updates to YouTube's community guidelines posted, and also news about contests. The blog's home page just includes entries for the current month, so you'll also want to review the archives. And to make sure you don't miss a new entry you can subscribe to the blog through an RSS feed.

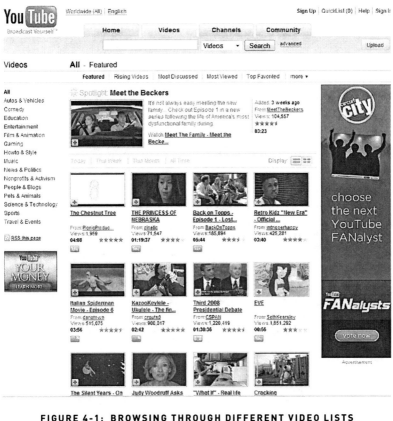

FIGURE 4-1: BROWSING THROUGH DIFFERENT VIDEO LISTS
ON YouTube IS FREE MARKET RESEARCH FOR PLANNING
YOUR OWN VIDEO.

You can add it to your Google home page, Google Reader, or your personalized Yahoo! page.

Set Your Goals

It's time for you to determine your own goals. Do you want to create a corresponding landing site viewers can click to after watching? Do you want to offer a coupon to reward those who click through? Do you want to build your brand? Do you want to gather subscribers to an electronic newsletter? Do you want to attract new clients or employees? Once you answer these questions, you'll be taking a big step forward in creating your videos. "If you are going to do YouTube videos," Paul D. Potratz Jr. of Potratz, a full-service advertising agency in New York, "you need to define what you want to do, for example, brand your business. Then, what is the viewer's next step? Where do you want to go from your video? If you don't specify this, it's as if you wrote only one chapter of a book."

Still, the beauty of YouTube is the low cost of entry into this marketing mecca. If you do it yourself, you can afford to make some mistakes as you learn your way around. To help boost you along, Steve Hall, founder of AdRANTs, an advertising industry blog focusing heavily on Internet marketing, shared some great overall advice. According to Steve, here's what commercials need to say:

- What the product or service is

- What it does

- Who it's for

- Why you would want it

With these elements in mind, Steve advises newcomers to "dive right in. . . . Throw videos against the wall and see what sticks!" It's great advice, especially because every video you create is a lesson in creating the next one.

Set Your Tone

There are a lot of low-quality videos on YouTube. They're poorly planned and badly shot, they have no goals, and they end abruptly. As YouTube caught on, videos filled the site, posted by people with no experience in videography who were using inexpensive equipment without any sense for the limitations of a five-inch screen. Many were put up just for fun. But simply because these kinds of videos are so prevalent, people often assume that lower-quality videos are still the way to go with YouTube. Actually, it's not as simple as that. (We know, what is?) Many people do find success with amateurish videos, but there are many videos that are much more polished and professional looking on the site now. As the medium evolves, and especially as people turn to it as a way to make money and advance their personal goals, we can expect the videos to continue to grow ever more polished and professional looking. Depending on what you want your videos to do, the more-polished approach may make sense as a better way to showcase your comedic or musical talents and boost your brand awareness with finesse.

Rather than planning an amateurish video, think along the lines of creating an authentic video. The quality doesn't have to be poor, but setting an authentic tone that resonates with your audience will go a long way on YouTube. "Video requires authenticity," explained John-Scott Dixon of Semanticator. "You can't fake it. It's the Blair Witch effect. YouTube audiences want reality." We've already seen that theory tested with the success of such campaigns as the *Penny Prankster* from OfficeMax.

Will You Do It Yourself?

Most individuals will start their YouTube adventures as do-it-yourselfers. In fact, many successful YouTubers have built their own presence on the site one video at a time. Companies, with full-blown public relations (PR) and marketing departments, may find they already have the staff, time, and resources to handle a new video venture. Only you can assess whether you have the resources to take on this task. If you decide your initial videos will test the medium for you, and if you have no greater goals in mind, you can start with something that you've already produced. Acadian Ambulance, for example, posted videos on YouTube that it had already created for other projects. "We did not lose any money or spend any extra money using YouTube besides the time it took a person to upload the video," said PR representative Maisa Dexler. Acadian's goals, while similar to those of many companies (branding and re-cruitment), were more modest in that they targeted primarily emergency medical personnel generally, and paramedics in partic-ular. They weren't aiming at the entire YouTube market.

Outside Companies Can Help

Remember that professionals are actually behind many of YouTube's famous viral videos. If an entire company wasn't behind them, select professionals still had a hand in producing them. You have a range of choices in working with outside resources. You can hire a company—for example, an advertising agency—to take on the whole project from concept through final editing and upload-ing. Or you may want to hire a company to help you with just part of the project such as concept design or editing. If you decide not to go with an established agency, you can hire key individuals—for example, a videographer or a writer—to help with the script.

Ben Relles, The Man behind *Obama Girl*

Ben Relles is the filmmaker responsible for the video *Obama Girl*. In the summer of 2007, when Barack Obama was polling at about 14 percent, Ben had a great idea. He created a now-world-famous viral video based on a beautiful young woman who had a huge crush on the young candidate. She danced her way throughout Manhattan explaining how deeply in love she was. He placed her on the subway, at the beach (next to a cutout standee of the candidate in the water), and even dancing on her desk at work. The initial idea came to Ben as a parody of *LonelyGirl15*, but he wasn't alone in creating this sen-sation. He hired a beautiful young actress to play the part, and he used a production team to shoot the video throughout the city.

FIGURE 4-2: BEN RELLES, THE MAN BEHIND *OBAMA GIRL*, FOUNDED HIS ENTIRE BUSINESS WITH THE LAUNCH OF THIS SUCCESSFUL YouTube VIDEO.

"I come up with the ideas," he told us, "but my main goal is to find the talented people to do the work. I find them through our own Web site [barelypolitical.com], Craig's List, or MySpace."

"How much time is put into a video doesn't correlate with success," says Ben. "That's pretty unpredictable." Ben has posted more than 100 videos in the year since *Obama Girl* launched his Web site barelypolitical.com. He had another big hit called *My Box in a Box*. Even though by then *Obama Girl* had skyrocketed him to fame, his production approach remained modest, although calculated. "I shot that on a $300 camera in four hours in Philadelphia," Ben told us. "I hired a $20-per-hour editor working four hours. People like to see videos that look like they could have done it themselves. That's better than a Hollywood image."

What Ben says is true, but let's not forget he brings a lot of relevant filmmaking background to the table. He knows how to assemble the best creative team he can for each project on which he works. You can too, not only through Ben's sources, Craig's List and MySpace, but also through Guru.com, where you can review candidates quickly and cheaply. There are also firms, such as Render Films, Woo Agency, and Giant Ant Media that will do everything for you, if that's what you want. Their charges vary, as you might expect.

Because interest in YouTube is growing so quickly and the site is becoming so much a part of everyday life on the Internet, you may be able to find a local advertising company that is willing to take on your project for a reasonable rate because they're looking for experience in online video. That's what happened when Moishe's Moving Systems of New York hired Drum Marketing and Public Relations to create the video *Crazy Mover Destroys Box of Wine Glasses*. The firm was looking for experience in creating YouTube videos and charged Moishe's only about $2,500 to $3,500—a bargain rate. The result for Moishe's was a video that helped it more than double its usual response to an e-mail marketing campaign. And Drum, of course, got the experience it needed to move forward with projects for other clients.

Of course, if you have deep pockets and are willing to pay for top, experienced professionals, they're out there. Render Films, for example, consults extensively with clients and then charges them the cost of production plus a margin. We were told that their average project is billed at $150,000 to $200,000. They work with clients such as T-Mobile and are also the agency behind the famous *In the Motherhood* Webisodes.

Finally, the people you work with don't actually have to be video professionals and may be as close as your own neighborhood. Film editor Chris Chynoweth of DropKickMonKey.com suggests that you consider whom you know and what they know. "Don't be afraid to ask the next-store-neighbor video whiz kid to edit your video or [ask] your friend who is a writer for a local newspaper to help you with a script," he suggests.

STORYBOARDING AND SHOOTING YOUR VIDEO

Your team is in place (or *you* are, at least), and you're ready to roll up your sleeves. What now? We don't blame you if you aspire to be the next *Dancing Man* or *Will It Blend?* or *Penny Prankster*. But come back to earth for a moment and save all that for your subsequent campaigns. The first time you rode a bike you didn't hop on a fully loaded high-tech mountain bike, which would be the envy of even Lance Armstrong, did you? Dennis the Menace's tricycle was probably more like what you pedaled. When making your video, aim for creating a mechanically sound film that does the basics right, and you will have served your purpose.

The place to begin telling your video "story" is with a storyboard. That's when you actually create a paneled comic-book-like board to show each scene you intend to shoot as you tell your story. How will you reveal the setting for your story? How many people will be required to make it happen? What props or costumes will you need for your players? All these details become much more apparent once you start building your story one panel at a time.

Equipment You'll Use

The basic equipment you'll need for your first efforts are probably close at hand, if you don't already own them. You'll need a camera or video camcorder and some editing software. Depending on where you decide to shoot your first video, you also may need some extra lighting. Finally, you'll need the computer you've been using all along to explore YouTube. Manufacturers of video cameras have obviously noticed the drive people have for capturing digital video easily and conveniently. Even your cell phone may have this capability. For the most part, an inexpensive digital camcorder or camera will be all you'll need to start out. You can always add more equipment as your experience level grows and you work on ever-more-complex productions.

VIDEO CAMCORDERS

Most video camcorders (see Figure 4-3) are inexpensive—some under $150—and easy to use. From our experience we've found that within minutes of opening the package, you can have a video filmed and uploaded to YouTube. It's that simple. Of course, that won't be the way you'll actually go about producing YouTube videos, because you'll be stopping for the editing process, but if you wanted to just shoot and share, you certainly can do it without any trouble. If the device has a handy built-in USB connector, and many do, that would eliminate even the simple need to have a separate attachment. Most

FIGURE 4-3: A VIDEO CAMCORDER (SHOWN HERE: THE FLIP MINO). MOST VIDEO CAMCORDERS ARE EASY TO USE AND ENABLE YOU TO POST YOUR FIRST VIDEO TO THE YouTube SITE IN MINUTES.

FIGURE 4-4: A VIDEO CAMERA (SHOWN HERE: THE KODAK ZI6)
IS A FULLY FUNCTIONAL VIDEO DEVICE THAT MAY EVEN
INCLUDE RECHARGEABLE BATTERIES.

camcorders run on batteries, and many are about the size of a deck of cards and probably don't weigh much more.

VIDEO CAMERAS

Increasingly, video cameras are becoming smaller and more portable and come with high-definition capabilities (see Figure 4-4). You will definitely need a memory card when you use some cameras, because they come with very little internal memory, but the card is inexpensive. Many video cameras provide easy uploading to YouTube, and some come with video editing software on a CD. The video camera is usually bigger than the camcorder but not so big that you can't slip it into a pocket. It also weighs more, but that's okay too. The LCD screens on video cameras are usually much bigger than the camcorders', and the price is a bit larger as well. A common standard configuration comes with a built-in USB, slow-motion playback, and precharged rechargeable batteries and a battery charger.

Filmmakers Classes Right on YouTube

You'll find plenty of help in making videos right in *The YouTube Handbook*. Everything from expert tips about storyboarding to all the steps that follow as you create your video are there. To get to the *Handbook*, click on the Help link, and then Video Toolbox, a link at the bottom of the page. Next, click on the Produce link, and you'll see links to videos and information on the following topics:

Camera Techniques:

- Nine Classic Camera Moves
- Panning and Tilting
- Using a Wheelchair Dolly

Lighting Techniques:

- Lighting Basics
- Lighting for Outdoors
- Lighting from a Single Source

Sound:

- Better Sound for Online Video, Part 1
- Better Sound for Online Video, Part 2
- Natural Sound to the Rescue

Special Effects:

- Green Screen
- Invisible Walker

- *Time Lapse*

- Split Screen

Using Webcams:

- Camera Placement . . . A Smosh Love Story

- No Lights, No Camera, No Action

- Webcam Video Effects

- YouTube Videos for Dummies

Spend some time in that part of *The YouTube Handbook* and you'll also see a clickable box from YouTube partner Videomaker. Click on it and you'll find other help available for the following subjects:

- Audio

- Editing

- Gear (All of these are in *The YouTube Handbook*, not the Videomaker Web site.)

- Lighting

- Pre-Production

- Shooting

Shooting Your Video

With all the help you'll find available in *The YouTube Handbook*, we feel reluctant to sacrifice more trees by parroting the good advice that's already so easy to find. The people we've spoken with who have been successful with YouTube have noted one thing specifically. That was to remember that you're shooting for a five-inch screen. We heard from many who told us that beginners often make the mistake of forgetting the limitations of such a small viewing field. You can't show wide expanses or complex and detailed scenes in such a small space. Shoot your video for your medium. For example, "focus on a landmark if you want to represent a geographic area," advises Amer Tadayon of Render Films. "If you want to do a shot of Wall Street, don't show the street, show the sign," he explained. It will much more quickly and effectively tell your viewer exactly where your story is set than a pan view up the street itself. Hetal Jannu and Anuja Balasubramanian of ShowMeThe Curry.com had some similar, good advice: "zoom in and show the details of what you are presenting." That approach is especially effective when they are presenting a new or challenging technique in the kitchen.

We are very far from claiming ourselves experts in video production. But, we are pretty clever when it comes to finding experts! We went searching for some qualified people to help us, and that's when we "met" Kevin Nalty, one of YouTube's most successful contributors. He's known simply as Nalts on YouTube, and he claims to be one of the site's least talented "cewebrities," but this is where we differ with Kevin. He's plenty talented, and the more than 700 videos he has listed on the site, along with the more than two million views his channel has received seem to prove us right. Kevin wrote a very helpful guide called *How to Get Popular on YouTube without Any Talent*. Here are some tidbits from Kevin's exceptional work.

How To Make Videos that Don't Suck, by Kevin Nalty

1. *Stick to your brand.* It's not sustainable to create content that doesn't reflect your personality, and it will confuse your audience. Find a unique style and stay with it. Know your audience and consistently provide for them.

2. *Short, Fast, and Big Finish.* Popular videos tend to be short, fast-paced, and offer a "big finish." People generally want two or three minutes, and 90 seconds might be ideal. It's much harder to edit a video to somewhere between 30 and 90 seconds, but it's almost always better that way. Sometimes I can't resist keeping some of my favorite moments, but I become infuriated with myself about undisciplined editing when I look at the video a week later.

3. *Have someone watch your video with you and note when they look bored.* You'll get a quick sense of what you can lose, and sometimes the best part of the video is what you left out.

4. *Topicality drives views.* Typically a major news event will spawn countless parodies, and timing is everything.

5. *Light your subject softly with lights on two sides, not ceiling lights that cast shadows.* Overcast natural light produces the best quality.

6. *Use an external microphone whenever possible.*

7. *Edit tight so most shots last fewer than five seconds.*

Editing Tools to Try

Wow. Kevin recommends a lot of editing. That means you'll have to know how to edit. Using an editing program might sound intimidating if you've never used one before. But remember that Hetal and Anuja from ShowMeTheCurry.com had never used editing software before either, and they both gained proficiency quickly. Video editing is hugely important, and perhaps more than anything, it is what separates a boring video from a compelling one. You want to give your audience the reward of the video without asking them to work too hard for it or wait too long for it. Remember, YouTube audiences are there to view lots of videos; making sure yours is concise and pithy as possible will increase the likelihood that people will watch it all the way through and share it with their friends. Length on YouTube is a factor, and not only because of the short attention span found among YouTube audiences. The site itself has a 10-minute limit on the length of videos you can upload. Most successful YouTube offerings come in under three minutes, and you should strive to keep yours well under that limit. In certain situations, say demo videos used by broadcasters, the video should be well under a minute, as that's the industry norm. If you think it's too hard to tell your story in so little time, go back and watch some of Kipkay's how-to videos. Many of those show every step of the task in as little as 45 seconds.

Luckily, video editing software has only gotten easier to use, and there's no reason to think that this happy trend won't continue. Let's take a look at some of the most popular video editing programs used by YouTube video creators.

MICROSOFT MOVIE MAKER (WWW.MICROSOFT.COM/WINDOWSXP/USING/MOVIEMAKER/)

This program actually comes bundled with newer computers that are running Windows. If you're running either XP or Vista, just go to Start, then Programs, and you'll see it right there waiting for you. The program is completely nonintimidating, with the screen split into just three main areas: panes, the storyboard/timeline, and the preview monitor. Click on the Help link at the top of the screen for a quick tutorial.

IMOVIE (WWW.APPLE.COM/ILIFE/IMOVIE/)

This is the movie maker program that Mac users favor. It's part of the suite of programs that comes with every Mac computer. It's got that great Apple interface that means you can accomplish things in such an intuitive way. Even though it's free, many people find it fully functional enough to make great videos. So if you're a Mac user, it should definitely be the first program you try.

ADOBE PREMIER ELEMENTS
(WWW.ADOBE.COM/PRODUCTS/PREMIEREEL/)

Adobe claims this software is the most popular video editing software on the market, which means either it's quite good, or Adobe does a great job marketing it, or both. You can make the software even more valuable by signing up for a photoshop.com plus "membership." It runs on Windows (XP or Vista), and costs about $150.

FINAL CUT PRO STUDIO
(WWW.APPLE.COM/FINALCUTSTUDIO/FINALCUTPRO/)

A favorite of many professionals, Final Cut Pro is Mac-compatible software that works with any kind of video. It includes extensive editing tools that let you smooth out shaky video, use 150 filters and effects, and easily preview your completed projects. This one is for the pros and the price tag—$1,300—is considerable. A less expensive version, Final Cut Express, is available for $199.

COREL VIDEOSTUDIO (WWW.COREL.COM/)

A bargain at $99 this video editing software lets you handle all the tasks you'd expect—editing, adding special effects and titles, but you can also paint, write, or even draw on your videos. A free trial version is available for you to test-drive the software.

YOUTUBE TOOLS

Right on YouTube you have access to a growing number of tools that make it easier to add features to your videos. For examples, you can add annotations, links, and chat bubbles with the new video annotation feature. These are so easy to use that you run the risk of overusing them to the point where speech bubbles, for example, become too distracting. Finally, you may want to experiment with more advanced video creation techniques such as mashups, or videos that are blended together from other videos. If so, there are Web sites to help you convert YouTube videos so you can work with them more easily when creating mashups. Check out, for example, Vixy.net and Zamzar.com. YouTube itself also has a remixer, allowing you to create mashups.

Acceptable Formats for YouTube Videos

Here are all the specs you'll need to make sure your final video is compatible with YouTube. This information comes directly from YouTube itself, and shouldn't be a surprise or problem for you. That's especially true if you use one of the newer YouTube-ready camcorders on the market.

- Video Format: MPEG4 (Divx, Xvid)

- Resolution: 640 × 480 pixels

- Audio Format: MP3

- Frames per second: 30

- Maximum length: 10 minutes (we recommend two to three minutes)

- Maximum file size: 1 gigabyte

Titles, Thumbnails, Annotations, Music, and More

Once you've shot and edited your video, you'll need to think about the title, which image from the video will serve as your thumbnail, and whether you want annotations within the video. The title is an important keyword tool to help your video pop up when people search for hot keywords. We'll spend a lot more time talking about titling as a means of attracting attention for your video in Chapter 5. The thumbnail, that still frame that pops up when your video is selected in response to a search query, may be the most important piece of advertising of all. Finally, an annotation allows you to make an additional remark "on the sly" to your viewers, an insider's comment that makes the experience more personal. Asa Thibodaux and Michael Buckley both use annotations effectively. You can also use the annotation feature to add a Web address to your video.

As for that all-important thumbnail, think carefully about what might be most likely to attract YouTube browsers and turn them into YouTube watchers. "Thumbnails come from the middle or the three-quarters mark of the video," explained Jay Grandin of Giant Ant Media. "The default [set by YouTube itself] is halfway through, and you can choose to change that to either one-quarter or three-quarters of the way through. At first we used a set of taps [for the shower video *Women vs. Men*]. I changed the taps to a custom thumbnail of Leah washing her hair. Now I get about 5,000 views a day." Jay speculates that the video gets the extra hits because some people click through thinking they'll catch a glimpse of a little more of a pretty young woman in the shower. It's not so, but that doesn't matter as much as the fact that this is what people think!

Annotations help you make remarks to your viewers, but they also allow you to include a Web address. That way, you can encourage your viewers to click through to your landing site where you can enhance the viewers' experience. There, you can either sell relevant items, offer an electronic newsletter, or even just encourage them to read your blog. In addition to annotating your videos, there are many ways to enhance your presence on YouTube; we'll cover many of them in Chapter 5. For now, just note how simple it is to use the annotation feature when you put up your video on YouTube.

Here is some helpful information from YouTube about adding annotations.

Adding Annotations to Your Videos
Couldn't Be Easier

YouTube offers you different options for adding annotations to your videos. To get started, sign into your YouTube account and choose the option that seems most suited to your needs.

Option 1:

1. At the top of any YouTube page click the Account hyperlink.

2. Where it says "Manage My Videos," click "Videos, Favorites, & Playlists."

3. Locate the video you want to add annotations to.

4. Click "Annotate Video."

Option 2:

1. On your Channel page click on the video you want to annotate.

2. Look to the right, you'll see a blue box that says "Video Owner Options."

3. Just click on the "Add/Edit Annotations" button.

We told you this was simple, but don't let the simplicity of this dissuade you from doing it, thinking this is "just too easy." It *is* easy, but it *works*. You can also add information about your company by including a screen at the end with your logo and the relevant link, as shown in Figure 4-5.

Even if you don't currently have a fully functioning Web site, you should still include a final screen to brand your YouTube channel. Simply branding your business or yourself—getting your

FIGURE 4-5: THE FINAL CLOSING SCREEN OF EVERY VIDEO
BEN RELLES OF BARELYPOLITICAL.COM ADDS TO ALL OF HIS
YouTube VIDEOS. NOW YOU KNOW EXACTLY WHERE TO FIND
MORE INFORMATION THAT RELATES TO THE VIDEO YOU JUST
ENJOYED.

name before YouTube's mass audience—is worthwhile even if it
doesn't directly lead to ringing cash registers. Ultimately, it will still
add coins to your coffer. It's the rare company or entrepreneur that
doesn't want to spread its brand before the public.

Royalty-Free and Copyright-Free Music

Although you may think that Bob Dylan or the Beatles, or a Cold Play song would set just the right mood for your video creation, of course you just can't incorporate it—at least not legally. And unless your budget is much bigger than we're assuming it is, you don't want to pay for the rights to use those songs either. Fortunately, there's a lot of royalty-free music available these days (music that doesn't require a fee be paid to the artist every time it's played), or copyright-free music that's available for nothing, no fee whatsoever. Just Google "royalty free music," and a wealth of options will appear before you.

Fred Light is one producer who has found that royalty-free music meets his needs just fine, although obviously it does limit his options. "Sometimes I buy the rights to a song," he told us. "I pay $75 to $80 for a song, but then I can use it repeatedly."

Posting Your Video

Posting the video is easy. Have you ever uploaded a video file to your computer? It's about as simple as that. Any YouTube page has an inviting yellow Upload button in the upper-right-hand corner of the page, shown in Figure 4-6. Click that, and enter a title, keywords, tags, and a description. YouTube will then ask if you want the video to be public, or private (meaning only select people can view it). Because you're looking to make money from your video, we assume you'll want to select Public. Click the Upload button again, and then, just as you would for a picture or file you wanted to upload, browse for the video's location on your computer. Click on that Upload button once again, and your video will soon be available on YouTube. When? The time it takes to appear varies from minutes to hours, according to YouTube.

If only ensuring that your video is seen by as many people as possible were as simple as uploading it! Sadly, it's not. To give your video its best shot at fame, you'll want to be selective when choosing a title and keywords, and when finishing up the details of your

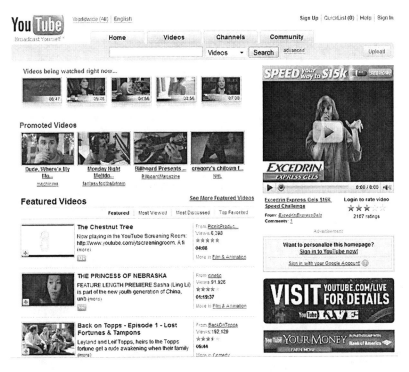

FIGURE 4-6: ANY PAGE ON YouTube WILL GIVE YOU A LINK THROUGH WHICH YOU CAN UPLOAD YOUR VIDEOS.

upload. This is all done from the Video Upload screen, shown in Figure 4-7. Let's consider each item one at a time.

TITLE

The title is the video's headline. It's the title that will either entice viewers to look at your video or convince them to pass you by. You want browsers to think to themselves that the video will either be entertaining enough or provide the information they need to make them willing to invest two to four minutes or more of their lives watching it. It's a good idea to go back to the site and browse through some videos again. What titles "pop" and make you want to click on the link? Which do you bypass quickly? You'll start to see patterns. Arnel Ricafranca of Fitness VIP boiled it down to this: "The title should be 'exciting.' Shocking can also work."

DESCRIPTION

YouTube has some excellent tips on creating descriptions for your videos. Most important is to make sure the descriptions are "clear and specific." They suggest you zero in on the content that will most distinguish your video from other videos. Sentence fragments are out. Instead, you should use descriptive language and complete sentences.

VIDEO CATEGORY

You'll also need to assign a category or appropriate topic area for your video. Use the pull-down menu and select the one that best fits your video. If you're unsure where to place your video, browse the site and see where videos similar to yours have been categorized.

TAGS

The tags (often referred to as keywords) you assign to your video are important because they can make the difference between someone finding an item when they search for it or missing it entirely. Think of the terms you might use when entering terms in the search box.

Choose your keywords carefully based on your video's topic and title. For example, let's say you've uploaded a video about solar energy. Tags might include "green energy," "wind power," "alternative energy," "green construction," "solar cells," and so on. Hetal Jannu and Anuja Balasubramanian of ShowMeTheCurry.com choose keywords plucked from their recipes. Arnel Ricafranca of Fitness VIP is an expert in his field, so he knows which words will get attention. For example, he knows to include phrases such as "How to build muscles" to his descriptions and tags. He must be doing something right, as his videos appear very high up in Google search results.

BROADCAST OPTIONS
Who do you want to be able to view your video? "Public" is the default.

DATE AND MAP OPTIONS
We're not sure why anyone would use the map option other than to check out another fun tool. But it does give you the ability to specify the exact place you recorded the video. Viewers will then see an associated map with the location pinpointed.

SHARING OPTIONS
These options include things like allowing viewers to post comments, vote on your video, embed it, and syndicate it. By default, all these things are allowed, and we recommend you don't change those settings.

As you get started producing video, remember you're supposed to be in a learning mode right now. Trying different things and making changes based on the view counts, comments, and any other feedback you receive will provide you with a real hands-on education. Few of today's YouTube stars were successful with their first attempts. You may find you change the title a dozen times or more. We'll spend the next few chapters helping you maximize your exposure on the site. YouTube's analytics will be a part of that and will help you get a feel for whether or not you're achieving your goals. You'll quickly learn what you might do differently next time. Perhaps that's the greatest thing about YouTube. It's so easy to add videos and so inexpensive to post. There can always be a next time. Every time you produce a new video, you complete another step in your own YouTube education. Just be sure to have fun along the way. And don't be surprised if you get way more hits than you thought you would.

WHAT I KNOW NOW

Here are some of the key takeaways from this chapter on how you can make YouTube videos:

- There's a lot of competition for attention.
- Before making a video, have a clear landing site in mind. Know just what the viewer is to do after watching the video.
- Plan the video based on what feels right for one's own personality or the company's corporate image.
- Plot the video on a storyboard first.
- Gain proficiency with video editing software.
- Edit videos carefully to tighten the message.

JUST FOR FUN

Here are some more YouTube videos we've enjoyed:

- *Bad Haircut Prank*
- *Food Court Musical*
- *Mall Pranks by Nalts*
- *Shane Sparks DVD Hip Hop Class*
- *Stork Patrol*
- Walt Disney's *The Story of Menstruation*

5

PROMOTING AND DISTRIBUTING YOUR VIDEOS

You have a video or two produced and a product to promote and distribute, but, in many ways, your work has just begun. To ensure that people other than just your family and friends see your video you'll need a plan. "I was taught in business school that you can't put a product on a shelf without telling a lot of people it's there," says David Mullings of YouTube's Realvibez channel. "In the same way you can't just upload your video and wait for people to come to you. Marketing plays a major role in kicking the snowball down the hill."

But the Internet is vast and mostly anonymous. How will you go about spreading the word about your work? How will you attract subscribers? What can you do to make sure your message is reaching the audience you've targeted? The answers lie with the insights and experiences of dozens of YouTube denizens who've figured this out for themselves and then were happy to share what they've learned with us.

First, take a deep breath and keep one thing in mind: this isn't brain surgery. To sell a product or service to someone, you simply have to get that person to notice it, give him or her something to remember, and present your case. If you've created a good video and targeted people you know might be interested, you'll find your audience. Blendtec's George Wright puts it this way, "You don't need to be on the front page of YouTube. You need to be on the front page of wherever your audience gathers. Isolate, identify, and become active in that corner of the Internet."

This is great advice, and we're about to show you lots of ways to accomplish this goal. But since it wouldn't *hurt* to make it to YouTube's front page, we'll cover that, too. The process of spreading your video around the Web is called "seeding." The term *seeding* sounds anachronistic when discussing the twenty-first-century phenomenon of YouTube video promotion. But if you want to be a YouTube success, you had better get used to it, whether you have a green thumb or not. Once you have properly seeded your videos, you'll also want to *fuel* them. Seeding gets momentum building for your video, and fueling keeps it going. "Our seeders get the buzz started," explained David Abehsera of the Woo Agency, "and our fuelers keep that going. Right off the bat our video [Sean Kingston's *Beautiful Girls*] went on around the world." When we last checked, more than 46 million viewers had enjoyed *Beautiful Girls*.

David Mullings is something of an Internet Johnny Appleseed when it comes to seeding. He has created successful YouTube campaigns involving such celebrities as Mariah Carey and Cezar, the first Reggae singer ever endorsed by Coca-Cola. David is only 27, but he's a YouTube veteran with tried-and-true techniques for marketing the videos he produces. David embeds his YouTube videos on the front page of his own Web site. "I embed the video on the front page of Realvibez.tv," he explained. "We get over 1,000 visits per day to the site, and even though we could run the video in our player, it doesn't generate nearly as much publicity as a hit on YouTube." David shared some of his favorite suggestions.

David Mullings' Video Promotion Steps

- Share the link on YouTube.

- Change your status on Facebook (e.g., to say you're uploading the video).

- Twitter about it. (Use Twitter.com to send the word out to the world.)

- E-mail the link to all the appropriate people.

- Message a select group of friends on Facebook and ask them to share it on their profiles.

- Post the link to the video in appropriate groups.

- Post the link or embed the video on appropriate message boards. And the secret sauce:

- Embed the video on the front page of your Web site.

You can see that David uses every tool at his disposal from Facebook to Twitter, to embedding video links, to old-fashioned e-mail promotion, and newer techniques like e-mail blasts. Let's begin by looking at the simple techniques first. Like so many other endeavors, we'll begin simply and build to more complex and diverse strategies as we go. By the time we're done with Chapter 5, you should already be seeing an increase in views with the videos you've posted. We're expecting you to take lots of breaks during this chapter so you can jump on your computer and get started right away making your work known to the world.

SIMPLE PROMOTION AND DISTRIBUTION STEPS

There are many different ways for you to begin seeding your videos. Along the way, you'll use blogs, e-mail blasts, even simple word of mouth. Ultimately, you'll want people all over the Web to know about your work, but, before you start spreading the word, we want you to see how far you can go just by promoting your work on YouTube itself. There is a lot of work to do right there at home, before you start branching out all over the "neighborhood."

Start with YouTube

YouTube offers you lots of ways to promote your video and make sure it reaches as many people on the site as possible. This part of the process is vitally important, because about 200 million unique users visit the site each month. Clearly, it makes sense to maximize your video's exposure right there. In Chapter 4, we covered the importance of choosing the correct category, title, and tags and writing a great description complete with the best keywords. All those things will help when users search for videos like yours. (Later in this chapter we'll discuss all this again as part of your search engine optimization efforts.) But first let's look at some other actions you should take on YouTube to promote your videos, your channel, and your brand. We'll also cover steps you should take to ensure that the work you've done stays as effective as possible.

Post Regularly and Often

It's important to post regularly, especially once you've begun to have a subscriber base. Your goal is to have fans who will be looking for your next video. If you fail to post new work, your subscribers will forget about you and move on to more regular contributors. While you have their attention, keep it and reward it with new work. Remember that chart from Chapter 4 that shows all the various media your videos compete with these days. It's vital that you maintain your share of your fans' mind space! Comedian Asa Thibodaux posts about four videos a week on YouTube. "Once you reach a certain level," he says, "it's kind of a balance between the number of videos and the number of subscribers." (Asa has more than 20,000 subscribers.) It's interesting that Michael Buckley, of *What the Buck?!* fame, gave us much the same advice. And he has more than 250,000 subscribers! He says that "the key for me now is creating videos quickly. I'm making three or four videos a week." To Michael it's about "staying in touch with your community," and the best way to do this is to keep posting videos.

USE THE SHARE OPTION

Your video will get its best exposure on YouTube for a very brief time—when it's just been uploaded to the system. When viewers click on a category link (say News & Politics) they can zero in on videos of interest by clicking on the hyperlinks across the top, which include Featured, Rising Videos, and Most Discussed. If they click the down arrow next to the more link, however, they can display Recent Videos. That would be yours, at least for a little while.

After that, you'll need to be more proactive. One of the best tools YouTube gives you to promote your video is right under your nose—or your video's nose, that is. It's the Share link that appears under your video when people view it. Click that, and one of the options you'll get is to "send this video." You can fill in an e-mail address in the box, or just highlight All Contacts or Friends, and YouTube will send it to the people on those lists. You become friends with other YouTubers, by the way, when they've accepted your invitation to do so. You send those invitations from your Channel page. And contacts consist of the list of people you've added to your address book. For more on how to use your address book and gather contacts, see the YouTube Help Center. The section on Sharing Videos is what you'll be looking for.

COMMENTS: LEAVE THEM OR REMOVE THEM

People can make any kind of comment they want about your videos, as long as you have allowed this feature when you uploaded it. That's fine. The comments can be quite amusing, spark further dialogue, and suggest how popular or provocative your video is. But did you know you have control over these comments? That's a good thing, because comments can work against you as easily as they can work for you. "You need to watch the comments that are posted for your video," advises Michael Parker of Serena Software. "Keep an eye out for unacceptable comments." What's unacceptable? Anything that's completely off target, such as spam pointing people to another video or site, something nonsensical, or comments riddled with typos and curse words. As much as we understand the temptation to remove all negative comments and just leave positive ones, we advise against that. The dialogue that can start when supporters respond to the negative comments can really boost your ratings. As Michael Buckley says in the beginning of each of his videos, "Rate It, Even If You Hate It!" You'll find all the help you need to manage your comments on YouTube's Help Center.

RESPONSE VIDEOS

A cool YouTube feature allows users to respond in video form to your video rather than with textual comments. Videos that have a lot of response videos are usually popular and provocative (there are those two *p* words again), and they will also attract the eye of browsers. We know of one agency that actually creates some of the response videos appearing in reaction to videos they upload for clients. That seems like gaming the system a bit, but we'll leave it to you to decide if that's a tactic you'd like to use. But response videos work the other way, too. Post your own videos as video responses to gain additional exposure. Just be sure to post them where they will be relevant, to avoid spamming and angering the YouTube community.

RELATED VIDEOS

It's all about getting more views, so if a thumbnail of your video happens to appear as a related video next to lots of other videos, you're seeding like a farmer. This happens if your video covers the same territory as other videos. It then appears to the right of those videos under the headline Related Videos. That means more exposure for you! We'd like to tell you exactly how to make sure your video appears under Related Videos for the site's most popular videos. But YouTube makes it clear that you have no control over when your video appears as a Related Video. They're selected based on "certain factors." Elsewhere on the site, YouTube notes that related videos are "selected by a mysterious search algorithm. They might be related to the video you're watching!" (This is cute, but not all that helpful.) Obviously, your video's topic, title, tags, and description help determine what other videos are related to it. So, choose them carefully. It's probably to your advantage that your video not appear as a related video if it's completely unrelated to the one someone is watching. Again, you don't want to annoy people.

SUBSCRIBERS, OR YOUR YOUTUBE FAN CLUB

Many of the promotional vehicles we'll discuss here all lead you to the same thing—building a fan base. Any celebrity can tell you just how important a fan club can be to their success. On YouTube your subscriber base is one big fan club, a club you want to build and cultivate. There are two steps to serving your fan club: building a subscriber list and then communicating with that list.

The people who comment on your videos are a great source of potential subscribers. Fitzy recommends that you "send them a comment back, or hit them back on their MySpace or Facebook." Doing that, he says, "means a lot to people." Another way to get subscribers is to just ask for them: encourage people to become subscribers to your channel right on your Channel page.

In the end it's the quality of your videos that builds your subscriber base more than anything. Michael Buckley has a knack for hitting all the pop culture hot buttons, and that has served him well. "A year ago I had 9,000 subscribers," he told us. Then, "I was featured on the front page of YouTube with *LonelyGirl15 is Dead!* That got me about 7,000 subscribers. It also got me the attention of other successful YouTubers. It's been a steady rise ever since."

Once you have a subscriber base, reaching out to them through tools like Twitter (discussed later in this chapter), and addressing them on your MySpace and Facebook pages helps keep them connected. How important all this is depends on the kinds of videos you offer. Comedians like Michael Buckley and Asa Thibodaux want lots of subscribers—the more the better. For Serena Software this objective is less important, as it's the quality of the leads they harvest that counts more than the sheer number of people who subscribe.

Making It onto YouTube's Home Page

This is the ultimate goal, of course, and will be the wonderful culmination of all your marketing efforts that preceded it. If you can make it to there, your video can make it anywhere. But, YouTube's editors determine what makes it onto the home page. One thing's for certain: it helps to have lots of subscribers or views. Once your video appears there, it will be as though Oprah Winfrey chose your book for her book club. Rockets will launch!

Make the Honors Roll

YouTube automatically tracks statistics for all the videos on the site. If any of yours are standouts, they will receive "honors" in categories such as viewings, ratings, how much they're discussed, and so on. Your overall channel can also receive honors related to the number of subscribers you have. Any of these honors will show up on your Channel page. *Will It Blend?* for example, has acquired the following honors for its channels and videos:

#35 - Most Subscribed (All Time)

#14 - Most Subscribed (All Time)—Directors

#31 - Most Subscribed (All Time)—Partners

#71 - Most Viewed (All Time)

#26 - Most Viewed (All Time)—Directors

#58 - Most Viewed (All Time)—Partners

Tooting Your Own Horn

As the saying goes: nobody loves a braggart. It's true, that jerk at the office who is always promoting his latest achievement can be hard to take. But somewhere between braggart and wallflower is the level at which all of us must represent what we do to those who may otherwise not notice. That's true of our daily lives, and it becomes even truer once you step onto a site like YouTube. You mustn't feel self-conscious about your work. If you really believed that what you had to say wasn't important, you wouldn't be making YouTube videos in the first place. So, tune up that horn of yours and get ready to toot. Don't be obnoxious about it, but if you don't champion the good work you're doing, you can't expect anyone else to do it either. Not only does the squeaky wheel get the grease, but it reaches its destination more comfortably, too.

Word of Mouth (WOM)

You may not think that talking about your work will make much of a difference. But, once other people start talking about your work, your views can climb quickly. It's not terribly different in our own line of work. As authors, we understand the need to promote our own work. With all due respect to our publishers, they have hundreds or thousands of books to promote, while we have just a few. Plus, we're the ones who spent countless hundreds of hours working on each manuscript, so it only stands to reason we have more of a stake in our own projects. Our advice to you is, if you're trying to build a business, be shameless about promoting your videos. Tell people about it; send it to friends and relatives, and notify your clients. It's your business, so get behind it 100 percent. Also, check out WOMMA, the Word of Mouth Marketing Association,

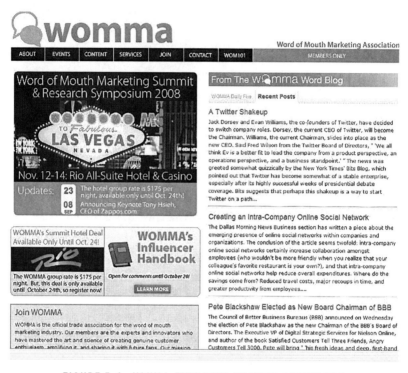

FIGURE 5-1: YOU'LL FIND LOTS OF GOOD ADVICE FOR
SPREADING THE WORD ABOUT YOUR WORK AT THE WORD OF
MOUTH MARKETING ASSOCIATION'S WEB SITE.

at www.womma.org, shown in Figure 5-1, for the latest techniques
in what was once thought the most provincial of marketing
methods.

Of course, thanks to the Internet and social networking sites,
you can also use your fingers to increase your word-of-mouth marketing. Jay Grandin's *How to Shower* video may have gone viral
without help from MySpace, but who can say for sure? One of the
first things that Jay did to promote his new video was e-mail it to
someone he knew at MySpace. MySpace then featured it on the
home page, and soon after that YouTube did the same. You can't expect the same reaction from the folks at MySpace to your creation,
but perhaps you know someone else in a position to promote your
video. This isn't the time to be shy.

E-mail Signatures

Why not include a link to your latest video as part of your e-mail signature? This bit of advice came to us courtesy of Hetal Jannu of the YouTube cooking show *Show Me the Curry!*. Links at that location are bound to get you some additional views. Be sure to change that link as you upload new videos. You might also want to include a link to your Channel page once you've really established yourself.

Business Cards

Business cards are cheap to produce these days. So why not promote your YouTube channel on cards you hand out (to everyone, of course)? Many online companies will offer to make up cards in bulk for a nominal fee, including shipping and processing (see Figure 5-2). The cost is usually a whole lot cheaper than what a regular printer would charge, and the paper quality is likely to be better also. What's the catch? The company's logo is likely to appear on the back of the card, at the bottom, in unobtrusive type. If you're creating and promoting videos for your company, business cards should be included in the budget you'll need to promote your videos.

Other Uses for Your Video

Use the video wherever appropriate—for example, within a presentation showcasing your company or yourself. Check to be sure all links are working properly, and make sure that the quality of presentation and content is right for your audience. You want to avoid any embarrassment at showtime.

Promote that New Video on Social Networking Sites

You're undoubtedly familiar with social networking sites; most people are nowadays. Basically, they are sites such as MySpace or Facebook where people with common interests may gather who may have never met up in another way. In fact, YouTube is a social networking site in the sense that it promotes communication via

FIGURE 5-2: MANY COMPANIES OFFER INEXPENSIVE
BUSINESS CARDS OF VERY NICE QUALITY, SUCH AS THIS ONE
FROM VISTAPRINT.COM.

the Internet among people with common interests. We're going to
focus a lot on video promotion on these sites because they are
where so much of the Internet traffic is right now, and they offer
so many opportunities for easy promotion. But years before there
was a MySpace or Facebook, Internet users gathered on message
boards through a system called Usenet.

While Usenet is definitely a Web 1.0 technology, many people still use it to communicate with others who share common interests. The easiest way to explore Usenet is through Google groups. (Click the More button on the Google home page to get to this area.) Amazingly, there are more than two million of these groups. Surely there are sites where groups of people gather who would be interested in your video's topic. Take some time to get the lay of the land, and if it seems as if members would be receptive to your message, post it, and include a link to your latest video.

MySpace

Your MySpace page is all about you or your company, so why not embed your YouTube creations into it? When you go to Michael Buckley's MySpace page at www.myspace.com/buckthehustler (see Figure 5-3), his latest YouTube video starts playing immediately. The

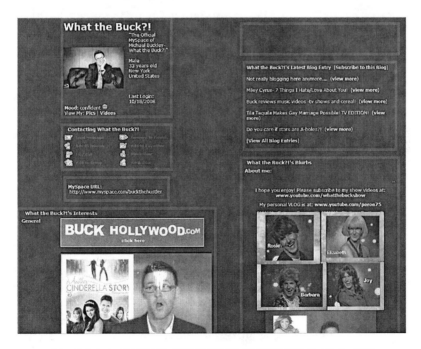

FIGURE 5-3: MICHAEL BUCKLEY PROMOTES HIS YouTube HIT
SHOW *WHAT THE BUCK?!* ON HIS MYSPACE PAGE.

whole site is geared toward promoting Michael's brand and his YouTube presence. His bio mentions that he's the host/writer/ producer of *What the Buck?!*, "the most popular show on YouTube." There's a clickable banner that takes you to a Web site where you can buy all sorts of *What the Buck?!* T-shirts and other merchandise. By the way, we got to Michael's MySpace page by clicking on the link in the What the Buck?! box from his YouTube Channel page.

FACEBOOK AND LINKEDIN

As with MySpace, Facebook allows you to post all sorts of items to your page, from links, to photos, to applications such as word games, to videos. So embed your latest video on Facebook, too. There's also another way to promote your new videos on Facebook: just click the Update Status button to let your friends know about the video, as in "Just uploaded a new YouTube video about how to get your book published." Every time you update your status your friends are notified when they log onto the site. New features, according to David Mullings from the Realvibez channel, make using status updates even better because you can use a sort that only shows you status updates. LinkedIn is an example of another social networking site with this sort of status feature. We get regular updates from LinkedIn about who's connected to whom and who's working on what. Mentioning your video in this context lets you easily notify people who have shown an interest in your work and what you're up to. David also updates his Blackberry status to do the same sort of updating and promoting.

TWITTER

Twitter sounds a lot like "fritter," as in fritter away your time. We admit, we never quite "got" what Twitter's appeal was until we researched it. Twitter (see Figure 5-4) is a social networking site that allows you to track the activities of your Twitter buddies through instant messaging, the Twitter Web site itself, or even a phone. If

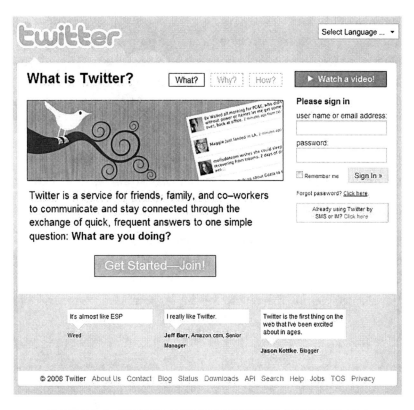

FIGURE 5-4: TWITTER LETS YOU NOTIFY YOUR BUDDIES THE INSTANT YOUR NEW VIDEO IS ON YouTube.

you're a Twitter subscriber, you're supposed to supply brief but frequent answers to the question: what are you doing?

What does all this have to do with YouTube? Twitter is another way to communicate with your fan base. If people choose to follow you on Twitter, they can receive your missives all throughout the day. That way, they can really feel connected to you. Michael Buckley announces on his YouTube Channel page that he "Loves to Twitter all day! Follow me!" But don't think Twitter is just for comedians; MBA holder David Mullings uses Twitter as one of his promotional tools when launching a new video. YouTube itself uses Twitter to provide its followers with "tweets on YouTube news, happenings, and featured videos."

StumbleUpon

StumbleUpon offers "stumblers" a unique proposition: tell the company what Web sites, videos, photos, and other Internet content you like, and its "personalized recommendation engine" will take that information and recommend similar content. After you register with the site, shown in Figure 5-5, you can add a "Stumble button" to your Web browser's toolbar. Then, you just click that button when you're on a page that interests you. From there you're taken to other pages that match your interests. StumbleUpon has an advertising program that lets advertisers target very specific audiences. When he was first launching his YouTube channel, David Mullings went to StumbleUpon/ads to craft a campaign to reach people he knew would be interested in his new channel. "When the Realvibez channel on YouTube launched, we spent $25 to get 500 people to our page," David says. He notes that with StumbleUpon he can target people

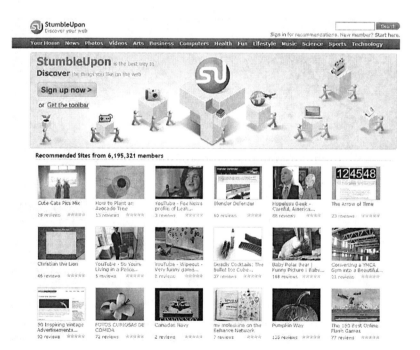

FIGURE 5-5: STUMBLEUPON HELPS YOU PROMOTE YOUR YouTube VIDEOS TO PEOPLE WHO SHARE YOUR INTERESTS.

by age, geography, and other criteria. Just make sure your channel's page and content are compelling, because those stumblers can rate it, and others will see those ratings. Of course, that's also input you can use to improve your page and content.

DIGG AND REDDIT

Make sure other social media sites such as Digg (http://digg.com/) and Reddit (www.reddit.com/) feature your videos. Digg and Reddit are examples of sites where users submit links to articles, videos, and other Web content that they find compelling. Other members then vote on the submissions, giving them a thumbs up or a thumbs down. If your video is good, it will receive both a lot of votes and a high percentage of positive votes, both of which will lead to many more views. So, to get things started, join these sites, if you're not already a member, so you can submit links to your videos. You'll be prompted for a title and description, and include the absolute best title and description you can. Don't send them every single video you produce, only the best. Sheer self-promotion is self-defeating on these sites: it's quickly spotted and strongly disparaged. Don't worry; once you expose your viewers to your best work, they'll likely seek out the rest of what you've done, too.

For other posting options like these, click that Share link we mentioned before. You'll see links to other sites such as Fark and Orkut. (No, we didn't make these names up, but thanks for thinking we're that clever.)

ADVANCED PROMOTION AND DISTRIBUTION METHODS

Now that you've seen the relatively simple steps you can take to promote YouTube videos it's time to dig into all this a bit more deeply. The more you dig, the more seeds you can plant. Besides, once you've taken all the steps we've just recommended, you won't feel like a neophyte in the world of Internet marketing. Look how far you've already come!

Fast and Easy Video Distribution through TubeMogul

TubeMogul is a company that provides market research information about the online video universe. It's very well regarded by many in the advertising and media industries. Most of the company's services are fee based. However, individuals can sign up for a free version of its video deployment service, which uploads your videos for you to up to 12 different video-sharing sites all at once. We'll have a lot more to tell you about TubeMogul and video-sharing sites in Chapter 6, but we wanted to tell you about this great free service as soon as possible. More information is at www.tubemogul.com/.

Organic versus Paid Seeding

The concept of seeding, like so many things these days, comes with organic and inorganic versions. Organic seeding is something you handle by e-mailing, posting to blogs you frequent, using Twitter, and even tools like TubeMogul's video deployment service. While it's free, as Christine Beardsell noted in an article for Clickz.com, there's plenty of work involved, too. If you have the budget, you may also want to hire an expert to do some inorganic, or paid, seeding for you. As part of this process, seeders will submit your video to the best blogs and forums, for example, and build a buzz worthy of a nest of bumblebees. In Christine's view considering all the competition on video sites these days, "some degree of paid seeding is a must if you want to rise above the clutter."

It all comes down to whether you have the time and interest to learn the skills and do the work yourself. If you have deep corporate pockets behind you, and your time is better spent doing other things, you may indeed want to hire an outside company to help seed your videos. Some companies to consider include Feed (feedcompany.com) and ViralManager (viralmanager.com). But we're going to assume you'll be doing the seeding yourself so you can become conversant in all the jargon, and what goes on behind seeding campaigns. That way, if you do at some point decide to hire professionals, you'll be an educated consumer of the services those professionals provide. In the meantime, a do-it-yourself approach may mean you never have a video that goes viral. But that isn't everyone's goal, anyway. Content producers like David Millings are still quite successful although they handle their own seeding and have yet to enjoy a viral video strike. Unlike Christine, David feels most people won't need to pay a seeding company.

YouTube Provides Insight

YouTube Insight is a free suite of tools that enables content producers to glean valuable information about the people who have viewed their videos. You can see the geographic areas those viewers were from and what time of day they viewed your videos. You can even compare how popular your videos are against other videos from a given region. To reach YouTube Insight, just mouse over to that magic Account link at the top of most YouTube pages, click the More link, and then click on the YouTube Insight link under Performance and Data Tools, shown in Figure 5-6.

As we wrote this book, there was only one link under Performance and Data Tools. YouTube has been planning further tools to help content producers learn more about how viewers were reacting to their videos and "engaging with them." On the drawing board are analytical tools that cover things like playback length, ratings, comments, and, most importantly from a marketer's viewpoint, the paths viewers take to get to your videos. Figure 5-7 shows the YouTube Insights Summary page for our account. As you can see, we were too busy writing this book to market our videos very

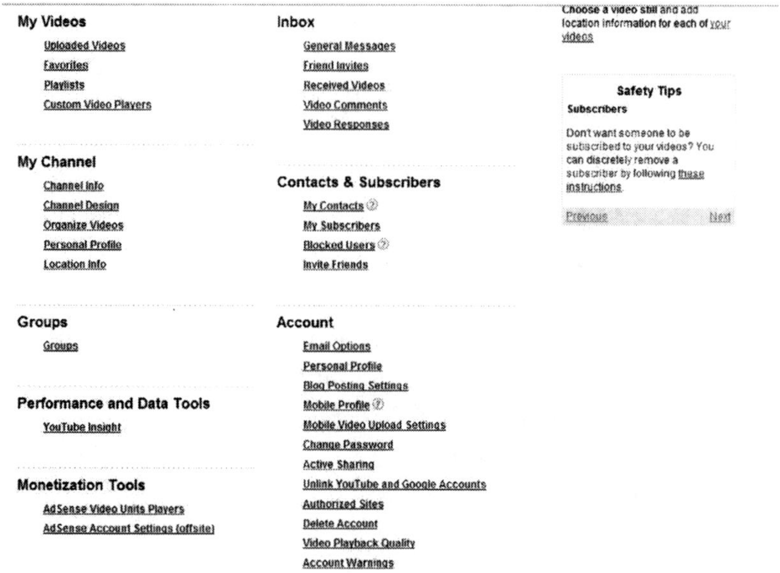

My Videos
- Uploaded Videos
- Favorites
- Playlists
- Custom Video Players

My Channel
- Channel Info
- Channel Design
- Organize Videos
- Personal Profile
- Location Info

Groups
- Groups

Performance and Data Tools
- YouTube Insight

Monetization Tools
- AdSense Video Units Players
- AdSense Account Settings (offsite)

Inbox
- General Messages
- Friend Invites
- Received Videos
- Video Comments
- Video Responses

Contacts & Subscribers
- My Contacts ⑦
- My Subscribers
- Blocked Users ⑦
- Invite Friends

Account
- Email Options
- Personal Profile
- Blog Posting Settings
- Mobile Profile ⑦
- Mobile Video Upload Settings
- Change Password
- Active Sharing
- Unlink YouTube and Google Accounts
- Authorized Sites
- Delete Account
- Video Playback Quality
- Account Warnings

Choose a video still and add location information for each of your videos

Safety Tips

Subscribers

Don't want someone to be subscribed to your videos? You can discretely remove a subscriber by following these instructions.

Previous   Next

FIGURE 5-6: YouTube INSIGHT CAN HELP YOU EVALUATE YOUR VIDEO'S SUCCESS AND GAIN VALUABLE INSIGHTS INTO HOW YOUR WORK IS STACKING UP AGAINST YOUR COMPETITION.

much! By clicking on the other tabs across the top of the page you can get more specific information about your video's views, popularity, and demographics for your viewers.

Sharpen Your Insights with Hot Spots

Flash! As we were working on this chapter, YouTube announced it was strengthening Insight with the addition of a new feature called Hot Spots, which shows patterns in how viewers watch their videos. Here's how the official Google blog describes them:

> The Hot Spots tab in Insight plays your video alongside a graph that shows the ups-and-downs of viewership at

different moments within the video. We determine "hot" and "cold" spots by comparing your video's abandonment rate at that moment to other videos on YouTube of the same length, and incorporating data about rewinds and fast-forwards. So what does that mean? Well, when the graph goes up, your video is hot: few viewers are leaving, and many are even rewinding on the control bar to see that sequence again. When the graph goes down, your content's gone cold: many viewers are moving to another part of the video or leaving the video entirely.

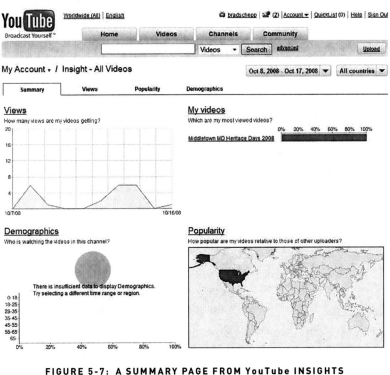

FIGURE 5-7: A SUMMARY PAGE FROM YouTube INSIGHTS PROVIDES A QUICK AND EASY LOOK AT SPECIFIC INFORMATION ABOUT YOUR VIDEOS.

Third-Party Companies and Tools

Given how fast online video is taking off it's no surprise that there are lots of companies offering to help assess your video marketing strategies and work with you to improve them. We've already mentioned Feed and ViralManager. Be sure to check out these companies whether or not you anticipate using their services. There are tips, articles, research highlights, and links on their sites covering video seeding, approaching bloggers, and nontraditional marketing. These are topics about which you want to gather all the information you can whether you're doing organic or inorganic seeding. Ramp Digital (www.rampdigital.com/) is another company to check out. They really get their hands dirty helping you not only target your videos but optimize your Web site so that when viewers wind up on your landing page they make your registers ring. Finally, with blip.tv (http://blip.tv/) you can create an easy-to-share video blog.

Blogs

Without exception, everyone agrees that if you want to get the word out about your video, if you want it to go viral, you need the support of bloggers. With more than 100 million blogs in existence, how do you pinpoint the ones to approach, and then how do you actually approach them?

TRACK BLOGS THAT MENTION YOUR VIDEO TOPICS
"Now that my video is on YouTube, I'm going to try to find as many bloggers as I can to post it," said author Samara O'Shea. "A friend of mine told me he knows someone on the Jezebel blog." (Jezebel covers topics of interest to women "in a substantial or humorous" way, and Samara's video about her book on journal keeping certainly fits in there.) Friends are just one way to locate relevant blogs. The most efficient way, though, is to do the legwork yourself. Your goal will be to locate blogs that cover topics related to your video's subject. You can do that by using tools such as Google's Blog

Search. When you search Google's Blog Search you may pull up many blogs, a lot of which won't be worth your time. To "vet" the blog, get a feel for its popularity and professionalism. Does it feature ads? Is it associated with other blogs you have heard of? Jezebel, for example, is part of the Gawker network of blogs, and Gawker is one of the most popular and well-respected blogs out there. Aside from Google's Blog Search also try one of the other blog search engines such as Technorati (www.technorati.com) and BlogScope (www.blogscope.net/).

Quicken Loans, the Cleveland Cavaliers, LeBron James, and an Etch-A-Sketch

Quicken Loans is the nation's largest online retail mortgage provider for reverse mortgages. In 2007 the company closed $19 billion in home loans. You wouldn't think that this is the type of company to try something as hip as a YouTube video, but they actually sponsored a video that had garnered more than two million views by the time we spoke with company representatives. We talked to Clayton Closson, Web content manager, and Matt Cardwell, director of e-commerce, at Quicken Loans. Both were thrilled with the results of their YouTube venture.

"We're a very traditional marketing company," Clayton told us. "We don't do unusual things. Here we're able to do that brandlike advertising without paying for all the exposure you'd get on TV. It's a lot more indirect." Timing, in this case, was just perfect. The owner of Quicken Loans happens also to be the majority owner of the Cleveland Cavaliers. The year of the YouTube experiment was also a year when the Cavaliers made it to the National Basketball Association (NBA) playoffs. A team representative discovered artist George Vlosich, who can do amazing things with the classic toy, Etch-A-Sketch. In this case,

FIGURE 5-8: LEBRON JAMES'S IMAGE SKETCHED INTO
AN ETCH-A-SKETCH GAVE QUICKEN LOANS A VIRAL
VIDEO SUCCESS.

he created a portrait of Cavalier star player LeBron James (see Figure 5-8). He brought the video to the Quicken marketing department. Rather than distribute it through more traditional media, such as TV, the group decided to give YouTube a shot.

They did some editing, deciding to brand it in the beginning and the end, but to eliminate the Quicken Loans logo that originally ran in a corner of the screen throughout the video. They wanted to avoid making the fascinating video into a "cheap ad." Once the editing was complete, the group got busy spreading the word. "We did a blogger outreach," Clayton told us. "We got some of the biggest bloggers to pick it up: Boing Boing, AdRANTs, AdAge. It really exploded!" Quicken Loans saw 300,000 views in one day! YouTube noticed and put the video up on their front page, quickly leading the view count up to a million. "We started to get calls from other companies asking how much we paid to get put on the YouTube home page," reported Clayton.

Part of the success of this YouTube venture was the blog outreach, and part of it was related to the fact that the video was tied to an ongoing event that already was attracting a lot of attention, the NBA playoffs. "I'm sure people saw that video and wondered who QL [Quicken Loans] was," explained Clayton. "Those months were some of the highest traffic months to our Web site. I wouldn't say one caused the other, but they *were* good months."

Build a Network of Bloggers

If you regularly upload videos on the same topics, you'll eventually build a network of bloggers who will get to know you. This network will always be evolving as the blogosphere (sorry, we tried to avoid using that term) grows and develops with new blogs appearing and others becoming inactive. In his tremendously valuable e-book, *How to Become Popular on YouTube (without Any Talent)*, Kevin "Nalts" Nalty gives some advice for content producers who want to reach out to bloggers. He suggests that they make it a point to become familiar with the blog and also personalize their notes to the bloggers. This may seem like common sense but it's so important we'll risk repeating the obvious.

List Building

Arnel Ricafranca's YouTube channel, IWantSixPackAbs.com, is one of the most successfully branded channels we've seen. While Arnel provides more than 140 videos that you can watch right on YouTube (see Figure 5-9), he also has multiple Web sites to which he directs

FIGURE 5-9: ARNEL RICAFRANCA USES HIS CHANNEL PAGE TO DIRECT INTERESTED VIEWERS TO HIS MANY YouTube VIDEOS, AS WELL AS TO HIS WEB SITES, WHERE HE CAN CAPTURE THEIR E-MAIL ADDRESSES AND ASK THEM TO OPT IN TO HIS E-MAIL CAMPAIGNS.

viewers through links on his Channel page and promotes right in his videos themselves. When we spoke to Arnel he was quite candid about the videos he posts to YouTube and their purpose: "I use the videos for list building. The bigger my list, the better I do. I e-mail the people on my list and send them some new videos to watch. When they watch my video, those videos will already be getting higher view ratings as they hit YouTube." Arnel knows that many of the people who visit his site won't buy anything the first time around. That doesn't matter to him, as he will still capture their e-mail addresses, so, as he says, "I can promote my products at anytime." He sends everyone on his mailing list a newsletter that promotes his Web sites and the added content that's only available to subscribers. "Within one year I had a little over 250,000 names on my list. I e-mail to it every week. If I had a traditional Web site where I didn't capture e-mail, I wouldn't have the chance to go back to them," Arnel said. He believes in the marketing adage that you have to see an offer seven times before purchasing.

E-Mail Blasts

Arnel is using the list he's built to do an e-mail blast. He's creating well-targeted e-mail campaigns sent directly to his customer base. If you decide to follow this path, remember that these aren't random e-mails. Your customers have opted in and agreed to receive your communications, plus you will include a link in every correspondence that allows those who receive your e-mail to quickly and easily change their minds and opt out. If you include a link to your latest YouTube video within an e-mail blast, you'll find a lot of your targeted e-mail recipients will gladly click through to see what you've done. You already know you're speaking their language. You're preaching to the choir, so you already have a solid chance for a good click-through rate.

To help spread the word about their new video *Moishe's Crazy Mover Destroys Box of Wine Glasses*, Drum Marketing and Public Relations sent an e-mail blast, shown in Figure 5-10, to Moishe's

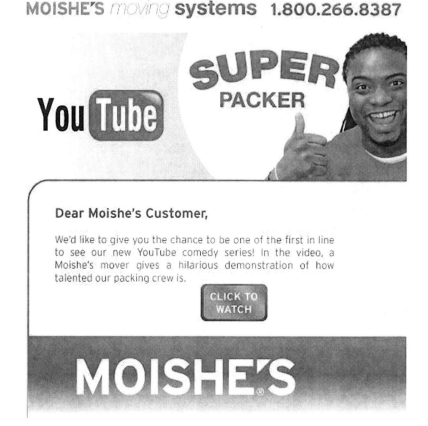

FIGURE 5-10: THIS E-MAIL BLAST FOR *MOISHE'S CRAZY MOVER DESTROYS BOX OF WINE GLASSES* REACHED MORE THAN 20,000 PEOPLE AND INCREASED TRAFFIC TO THE MOVER'S WEB SITE.

and their own customers. All told, the blast reached about 20,000 addresses. Including a link to the video really boosted their typical click-through rate. In fact, they had their most significant click-through rate ever, more than doubling what they normally get. Also, more people than usual went to Moishes.com during the first week of the video e-mail campaign. The promotion reverberated beyond the initial push. "Customers now say they have seen the video when they call to book," said Ryan Adler of Drum. Why not consider a blast of your own?

Should You Run a YouTube Contest?

YouTube encourages video contests, knowing full well they draw lots of views and even media attention for the site. Companies pay YouTube to set up official contests, and in return they get help with promotion and administering the campaign. For example, YouTube will provide you with a "contest gadget" (a small software application) that you can embed in your own Web site to help drive viewers to your contest.

To explore contests further, start by checking the Contests tab, located in the Community area. On the Contents page you can get a feel for what contests are like by reviewing both contests happening right now and those that have already passed. Official YouTube contests include four phases: Announcements, Submission, View & Voting, and Results. Interested? Click the Advertising link at the bottom of YouTube's home page to download PDF files about partnering with YouTube, including one about running contests. Of course, there are also many unofficial contests that are not part of the YouTube program. Driving traffic to one of those and handling the rest of the process will be up to you.

H&R Block and the "Me and My Super Sweet Refund" Contest

In January 2007, H&R Block began its "Me & My Super Sweet Refund" contest. We spoke with Paula Drum, vice president of digital tax marketing, about the experience. The contest launched on January 25, 2007. "We generated over 125 video submissions with more than two million views of TaxCut-related videos and more than 1,100 subscribers to the contest channel," Paula told us. "In fact, one of our seeded launch videos, *Candy*, held the record for nearly nine months on YouTube as the 'most-linked comedy video' of all time and the third 'most-linked video' of all time." Paula said that the video submissions ranged from song parodies to exercises in amateur special effects. They were creative, funny, and entertaining, while depicting what people would do with their tax refunds. How did this all work?

"We let the YouTube community select the winner. The YouTube community voted on the video submissions and chose the first-, second-, and third-prize winners. Voting began at 12:01 a.m. on February 23, 2007, and ended at 11:59 p.m. on March 23, 2007. We did validate that the videos met the stated requirements: one to three minutes in length and contained the key phrases: 'TaxCut Online' and 'Super Sweet Refund.' We also screened the video submissions for obscenity and other inappropriate content—after all, this was a PG-rated contest. What we hoped for were creative responses, and we received that!"

We asked Paula what the company's YouTube strategy is today in addition to this successful contest. "We look at all of our social media outreach, including YouTube, as a longer-term strategy, not a one-year marketing campaign," said Paula. "We are looking to longer-term measures such as brand awareness and brand attributes, positive word of mouth, and increased customer retention. Other indicators that we look at are how many people are interacting and engaging with the different social media tactics." Paula noted that "we look at a community and tailor our program in a way that we feel is appropriate for the community. The wonderful thing about communities is that they change over time, too. We strive to keep all of our activities relevant to the community at that point in time."

Video Search Engine Optimization

Search engine optimization (SEO) is a set of techniques designed to ensure that your Web sites—or, in this case, your videos—appear within the very first couple of pages of search results. That's where you'll get the most attention and the best click-through rate. SEO for videos is called "video SEO." If you don't use these video SEO techniques, your video will be like a single snowflake in a snowstorm, getting lost amid all the other flakes. With successful video SEO, you'll make your videos very easy to find, like red mittens are when they stick out of the snow. You know that when searching Google you're much more likely to click on anything that appears on the first page of results. Everything else beyond that comes to your attention only if you're already frustrated in achieving a quick search result. Your goal is for both regular search engines such as Google or Yahoo! and specialized video search engines such as Google Video Search and Blinkx to find your videos and rank them highly.

Once again, quality is where it all begins. Great videos get ranked higher, so achieving higher search rankings provides further incentive to produce dynamite videos. If you've created a compelling video and posted it to blogs and relevant forums, then there should be a lot of other sites linking to your video (these are called "inbound links"). The more inbound links, the merrier. "Having good content will jump-start a link-building campaign because at the end of the day people will always want to share/post/link to content they find interesting," notes Kieran Hawe in an excellent article appearing on Webtribution.com. That helps increase the number of inbound links from other Web sites, in turn increasing the traffic and ranking of your video.

Another way to achieve high rankings is to "optimize" the title, tags, and description you provide for your video. Your video's title should be both a "grabber" and at the same time culturally relevant. For example, in mid-2008, the United States was in the midst of an historic presidential election. It was difficult to find a featured, recommended, or most discussed video that wasn't political. But, that didn't mean you should have invented keywords or included irrelevant topical words in your titles. And that dictum still applies. For example, although it may seem that adding the tag "Lohan" to your video will get you a lot of extra views, those views aren't worth having if Lindsay Lohan does not appear in or is not mentioned in your video. If you attract viewers by misleading them, they'll note their disappointment in the comments they leave for you and the rankings they assign your video. Those extra views you had hoped for can easily turn into weapons that torpedo your success. And search engines are also getting wise to this practice, so videos that grow popular when they shouldn't are not necessarily rewarded with higher rankings. Search engines may actually penalize you for misleading viewers by ranking your video lower. Terms that you use should reflect all the most compelling aspects of your video's content. Tennis videos, for example, should include your name, tennis, sport, perhaps the name of the racket you use, but also what makes your video unique such as your United States Tennis Association (USTA) ranking (if applicable), forehand, backhand, serve (try aces), crosscourt shots, and so on.

The process described in this chapter isn't a one-shot deal. Instead, it's a continuing activity. Promoting your videos, and therefore promoting you, your business, or both, should be something you do, in one way or another, every day. You need to constantly monitor your video views and use tools such as YouTube Insight to see what's working and what isn't.

And don't forget the importance of genuine content and well-done videos. There's a growing backlash against people going all out to make their videos go viral, despite the video's content and whether or not the person being told about it would be interested in it. Video spam is no better than any other kind. In fact, it can be worse; it takes longer to view a video than it does to read an e-mail. In Chapter 6 we'll look more closely at how you can turn all this work—the creation of your videos and your promotion and distribution of them—into money.

WHAT I KNOW NOW

Here are some of the key takeaways from this chapter on promoting and distributing your material:

- Understand the concepts of seeding and fueling videos.

- Regularly post new videos to YouTube, which will help build a subscriber base.

- Use all of YouTube's resources to promote work, including comments and response videos.

- Don't be bashful about telling the world about a venture. Toot the horn!

- Explore appropriate social networking sites to find new ways to promote videos.

- Blogs that relate to video content can be very helpful in promoting work; find them.

- In time, decide about sponsoring a YouTube contest.

JUST FOR FUN

Here are some more YouTube videos we've enjoyed:

- *Eddie Izzard: Cake or Death*

- *How to Thread Your Eyebrows (by Eily311)*

- *John Coltrane—My Favorite Things—1961*

- *Nureyev & Fonteyn Romeo and Juliet*

- *Sean Kingston's Beautiful Girls*

6

YouTube: YOUR NEW REVENUE STREAM

YouTube is great fun—and a worldwide pop culture phenomenon. It is part of everyday life for millions of people. But, the question is, can you use YouTube to make any money? We asked a prominent YouTube partner about the connection between money and YouTube. He told us what we'd already suspected: "As for making money, that is always the tricky part."

Making money *always* seems to be the tricky part. But there are some strategies for making money with YouTube videos that clearly work. Throughout this chapter we'll look at both proven and up-and-coming strategies for making money on YouTube. Some of these we have touched on already, such as the concept of using your YouTube videos to drive viewers to a landing page. We'll introduce others, such as Google AdSense for video, for the first time. Before you reach the end, you'll see lots of examples of how people are generating revenue from their YouTube efforts, and you'll be armed with some suggestions of your own to try.

But first, what, exactly, is meant by "making money"? Sure, you or your company make money when you actually sell your products or services, and YouTube videos can help there. But getting your name in front of thousands of people in a positive way has value, too. That helps your branding efforts, and that should count as "making money" also. And so should the money you save on customer service, on recruitment, and on other forms of advertising because you're using online video and you're using it well.

The Internet has evolved so quickly in such a short time. While the money online video generates may be miniscule right now, is there anyone who would argue with the premise that the figure will grow exponentially? After all, as a society we love video. And the Internet gives us more control and more selection over our favorite form of entertainment.

You're still very much a pioneer if you're looking at ways to make money from online video. You're also an entrepreneur whether you operate as one independently or within a company, and you should think like one, advises Realvibez's David Mullings: "If a person is trying to make money from their online video, they are an entrepreneur, so they need to act, think and speak like one; otherwise they are just 'trying a thing' as we Jamaicans say."

YouTube's PARTNER PROGRAM

Just because you're an entrepreneur doesn't mean you have to go it alone. Why not have YouTube as your partner?

FIGURE 6-1: *AVRIL LAVIGNE—GIRLFRIEND* VIDEO REPORTEDLY EARNED AVRIL LAVIGNE $1 MILLION JUST FROM YouTube.

The *Avril LaVigne—Girlfriend* music video, shown in Figure 6-1, is now YouTube's number one most-watched video, with 100 million views and counting fast. Nettwerk Management, the music label and management company behind the video's distribution, has been widely quoted as estimating that the video will earn LaVigne $1 million from YouTube alone, as of mid-2008, thanks to YouTube's revenue-sharing program. We don't know if this figure will actually pan out—it's been questioned—but we do know that the money YouTube is paying out is very real, and in some cases not insubstantial.

As discussed in Chapter 1, to make real money on YouTube, you simply have to be part of its Partner Program. The details about how you qualify and what you can expect to earn are shrouded in secrecy. Apparently, becoming a partner isn't easy, but if your videos attract a lot of views, and you have lots of subscribers, you may be surprised at how quickly YouTube contacts you. Qualify to become a partner and all will be revealed—or at least all you'll need to know about your own income potential.

If you're a YouTube success, the company is absolutely the first place you can expect to turn for earning real money. And this advice goes beyond the Partner Program. With one of the world's busiest Web sites, and the world's second busiest *search engine* behind only Google's, YouTube is where the people are. It has the most traffic by far of any video-sharing site, and it therefore offers you the best opportunity to make money in lots of ways, all from your videos.

REDIRECTING: SELLING SOMETHING VIA LANDING PAGES

Suppose that someone is watching your video on YouTube. In essence, they've walked in the door to *your* shop. You have them captive, at least for the moment. Your job is to make sure your video is entertaining or informative enough so that the viewer sits through the whole thing and then wants to know more about you or your company. How are you going to turn that prospect into a source of revenue? Put another way, what is it that the video wants people to do?

One of the popular ways to turn viewers into buyers is to direct them to a landing page or microsite (discussed shortly). Again, we've mentioned landing pages briefly, but now let's consider them in more detail.

With a landing page set up you've provided a path, or what Steve Hall of AdRANTs calls "a call to action." This path may take the form of another site where you have items for sale such as DVDs, white papers, T-shirts—whatever is relevant to you and your business. Every chance you get you should encourage people to go to your landing page.

Diddy and his music label Badboyrecords have posted more than 200 videos to YouTube. His YouTube channel, branded "Diddy

FIGURE 6-2: DIDDY'S CHANNEL PAGE INCLUDES A LINK TO HIS WEB SITE (SEE THE BOTTOM OF THE "DIDDY TV" BOX).

TV" and shown in Figure 6-2, is thoroughly captivating and provides plenty of material for his fans to check out. Prominent on that page is a link to his official Web site, www.diddy.com. Click on that link, and you'll find CDs for sale (naturally) but also Diddy ringtones. There are opportunities to connect with other Diddy fans via a message board. And you can also feel more connected with Diddy himself by downloading Diddy wallpapers and buddy icons, and reading the latest news about him. Now, don't think Diddy sits at a computer all day programming these things; nevertheless, his YouTube presence and how his staff uses it to propel fans to a well-crafted landing page can teach anyone a thing or two.

Microsites

A microsite is a type of landing page that's particularly popular among online video producers. It's a special Web site created to support an online video campaign. WillItBlend.com, for example, is a microsite that supports Blendtec's *Will It Blend?* videos (see Figure 6-3). On Blendtec's YouTube Channel page there's a "connect with Blendtec" box, the highlight of which is the link to its WillItBlend.com microsite. From this site you can order your own blender, order accessories, and get recipes of many varieties.

FIGURE 6-3: WILLITBLEND.COM'S WELL-BRANDED MICROSITE SUPPORTS ITS YouTube VIDEOS.

FIGURE 6-4: BROCADE SOFTWARE HOSTS THIS DYNAMIC
MICROSITE TO ENTICE POTENTIAL CUSTOMERS AND GAIN
SALES LEADS.

Render Films set up a microsite to support its video campaign for its client Brocade Software: www.wantyourlifeback.com. On the site, shown in Figure 6-4, you can learn more about Brocade's products. This is also where Brocade collects qualified leads. Render's motto is "create the site you can control [the microsite] and drive traffic to it." Simple advice is sometimes the best advice.

David Mullings and Realvibez.tv

David Mullings started his first company at the age of 20, while working toward his MBA degree at the University of Miami. David graduated from college at the age of 19 and took some time off to play semiprofessional soccer. Then he

FIGURE 6-5: DAVID MULLINGS IS A YOUNG
ENTREPRENEUR WHO IS FINDING SUCCESS BOTH ON
YouTube AND ON THE WEB AT LARGE.

got to work in earnest, building his business with the help of his brother. Realvibez.tv is an Internet home for those who love Reggae and other kinds of Caribbean music. David is quite sure that his success on YouTube has made his business grow more quickly than would have been possible if he'd stuck to his own little corner of the Web.

As it happens, David's channel represents the first Caribbean media partnership YouTube made. "We have a revenue share deal just like other partners," David told us. But, in addition to the success he's found on YouTube, his partnership with the site has led to other very lucrative deals and offers. David was kind enough to share a few with us.

"We just closed a deal with one angel investor for $25,000 at a valuation of $500,000, mainly because of securing this YouTube deal," he said. "The channel will also serve as a major opportunity to expose our brand to a much wider audience, and we already have a unit of the Jamaican government willing to support the filming of content in Jamaica. The YouTube deal has opened countless doors, and we will be working closely with some of the top Reggae acts, like Sean Paul, to create and monetize our content."

David also told us a story about leveraging his YouTube exposure in a different way. In 2007, David decided to experiment with YouTube by uploading an interview he'd done with an artist by the name of Collie Buddz who is under contract to Columbia Records. He received the following message:

> I am an intern with Columbia Records, and I work for Collie Buddz. My job is to gather content for his updated Web site, which will hopefully contain various rare videos, interviews, performances, etc. I really like your interview with Collie Buddz, and I was hoping to use it for our Web site. Would you be willing to send me a copy of the file? Of course, you would be given credit and your name would appear on Collie's page.

"Naturally, I sent the video to them," said David, "and they have sent us promo items to give away on college campuses and via the site." The exposure has done wonders for David's young business. "I couldn't have called Columbia and gotten anywhere, but by uploading a video to YouTube, we got *them* to come to us and establish a relationship! Thanks to YouTube, I can call up a major record label, because they know us."

In addition to the success David is enjoying in the highly competitive field of music, he's also been speaking with Harvard's director of content. Let's remember that although David started his enterprise at the young age of 21, he's already seen this level of success, and when we spoke he was only 27!

VIDEO ADVERTISING

Another way to make money from your video is to earn advertising dollars from it. Online video advertising, like other facets of Internet advertising, has evolved and gotten more sophisticated. It's not just about placing commercials online instead of on television. The International Advertising Bureau (IAB), www.iab.net, has some thoughts about all this.

The IAB has defined four standard formats for in-stream video advertising (in-stream is the kind YouTube offers): pre-roll; interactive pre-roll, which invites the viewer to click a button to make something happen; overlay ads; and non-overlay ads.

Pre-rolls take over the entire viewing screen and usually play for a while, say 15 to 30 seconds, before the video starts. Pre-rolls may also run in the middle or at the end of your video. Overlay ads run concurrently with the video, usually at the bottom of the screen. The non-overlay versions of these ads still run concurrently. They run "outside the live video frame but within the video window."

This whole area is so new that what works and what doesn't is wide open for discussion. There's been concern that viewers are not willing to sit through pre-roll ads, in particular. You can rest assured that there are compelling reasons though for advertisers to run such ads against your content. The online ad firms Break Media and Panache did a comprehensive study of video advertising, testing the effectiveness of these ads. The study involved what the ad firms felt was a representative sampling of companies: truTV, Honda, and T-Mobile. They found that 87 percent of viewers were willing to sit through pre-rolls in order to see their content. "Pre-rolls are amazingly compelling," they reported. For overlay ads, the percentage willing to sit through them was still very high: 77 percent. These numbers also reflect how relevant the ad is to a particular demographic, a key point of great importance. Generally, younger

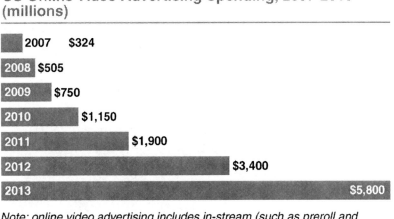

US Online Video Advertising Spending, 2007-2013 (millions)

- 2007 $324
- 2008 $505
- 2009 $750
- 2010 $1,150
- 2011 $1,900
- 2012 $3,400
- 2013 $5,800

Note: online video advertising includes in-stream (such as preroll and overlays), in-banner and in-text (ads delivered when users mouse over relevant words)

Source: eMarketer, August 2008

097113   www.e**Marketer**.com

FIGURE 6-6: U.S. ONLINE VIDEO ADVERTISING SPENDING.

audiences are more likely to sit through pre-roll ads than are older ones.

If all of this evaluation of the demographics seems like a lot of work, rest assured it's worth it. In August 2008, eMarketer released the results of its research, shown in Figure 6-6. Those results show the payoff is coming and it's coming big. Right now, online video advertising comprises just 2 percent of the money spent for all Internet advertising. That number will increase dramatically, according to the online market research firm, from about $505 million in 2008 to $5.8 billion by the end of 2013. For added perspective, by 2013 total Internet advertising will approach the advertising dollars spent on television.

Keep in mind that right now (or at least, as we're writing this) video advertising of the kind just discussed is not a big revenue stream for anyone. And "anyone" includes the companies behind such hits as *LonelyGirl15*, *Ask a Ninja*, *Republicrats*, *Wainy Days*, and Dr. Horrible's Sing-Along Blog, and any other viral video or Web series you could name. Even though these shows have received millions of views, and are distributed in some cases through multiple video-sharing sites all over the Web, the actual money they bring in is modest. The magazine *Fast Company* recently shed some light on the numbers by analyzing them: "With a $10-per-thousand-view ad rate, not uncommon in this market, a video that attracts 1 million views—a colossal hit—generates only $10,000." However, research firm e-Marketer feels the future looks much brighter for content producers looking to generate income from the kind of video advertising discussed here.

Google AdSense for Video

As YouTube's parent, Google should have figured out a way to incorporate its AdSense program into its video-sharing site. AdSense is the advertising program that turned Google from a simple search engine to a money machine. Through AdSense, Web site owners can have Google select ads based on the site's content, and then place those ads right on their sites. They do nothing except sign up for the program and collect checks, as people click on the ads. "We have had amazing success with YouTube, wrapping some video eye candy into our branding," says Patric Douglas of Shark Diver. "Thus far, 108 million views and counting: that translates into $90,000 in Google AdSense clicks." There are two types of ads available through Google's AdSense for Video program: InVideo and text overlays.

The InVideo ad program places relevant ads in the form of companion videos (actual embedded video ads) along the bottom 20 percent of the viewing screen. One ad appears per viewing, and the viewer can choose whether it is run at its full size or it collapses by clicking the "x" in the corner. Either way, the ad minimizes automatically after a few seconds. Text overlay ads are drawn from Google's advertiser network and are another way for you to earn money from advertising Google places on your viewing area.

Instead of placing videos, however, this program places those familiar Google text ads along that same part of the viewing screen. The words "Ads by Google" also appear. Ten separate text ads appear along the bottom of the screen and run for 20 seconds each while the video is playing. As with the video ads, viewers can choose whether or not to see the ads, again by clicking on the "x." If a viewer clicks on any of the ad's text, another window opens to display the full-blown advertisement. After the video has ended, three other relevant text ads appear on the Video Watch page.

If you own a Web site, microsite, or very popular blog, you can earn AdSense money from your embedded videos. You will need to meet Google's thresholds for how many videos you stream a month. To learn more, click on Advertising Programs on Google's home page and follow the digital breadcrumbs starting with the link Google AdSense, appearing on the right-hand side of the page. Before you apply, give some thought to how adding AdSense ads will fit in with your overall business goals. Obviously, you may not want to clutter up your company's Web site or microsite with text ads, or even have an ad run prior to the start of your video. By the way, if you're in YouTube's Partner Program, you're all set: AdSense is included, and video or text ads will automatically appear with your videos.

AdBrite

AdSense for Video isn't the only service available that automatically places advertiser's ads in your videos. A company called AdBrite offers a similar program called InVideo (the same name that Google uses!). Through this program, AdBrite will place interactive text ads within your videos, whether they appear on your Web site or blog or are embedded on other sites. "The ads are not intrusive and disappear within a few seconds," says a company representative. The AdBrite program will also allow you to brand your videos by placing your logo in them. For more information, go to www.adbrite .com/mb/.

Sell Your Own Ads

Would you rather line up advertisers yourself? If you are a "professional content producer" and have an ad sales team, *you* can sell ads that will appear alongside your YouTube videos, according to *Advertising Age*. You and YouTube will split the income 50/50. There's not much information on the Internet about the program. "The program is not well publicized," Google public relations representative Adam Zamost told us. "Although it's true," he added, "that we do work with partners in this fashion."

This program makes it seem like you're doing all the work while YouTube sits by and collects 50 percent of the revenues. It's worse than having an agent! But, remember how many viewers YouTube drives to your content and ads. Also, if you make the deals with advertisers, you have a lot more control over which ads appear on your page. Through the AdSense program you have no control at all, because it's Google's algorithms that determine which ads will appear.

As Adam elaborated:

> Our goal is to help media companies explore different ways of generating revenue from their content. Many partners can leverage the strength of their own sales forces to package together all their content, no matter where it's distributed online (including YouTube). This is a valuable option for some, but not all partners.

For more information, start with YouTube's Partner Information page at www.youtube.com/partners.

TubeMogul's Dating Service: Matching Video Producers with Advertisers

You have video; advertisers have money. Aside from programs like Google's AdSense, how do the two of you hook up? Through the "matchmaker," the Internet video consultant TubeMogul. It has created the TubeMogul Marketplace, which was just getting underway as we were writing this book. The purpose of this new "dating" site is to connect video producers with advertisers and even investors looking to get into the online video field. The Marketplace is slated to include previews of "Web shows," profiles of the content producers, and information about the demographics of the audience. The company announced that any TubeMogul user could establish a profile. See Figure 6-7 to get a better feel for this service.

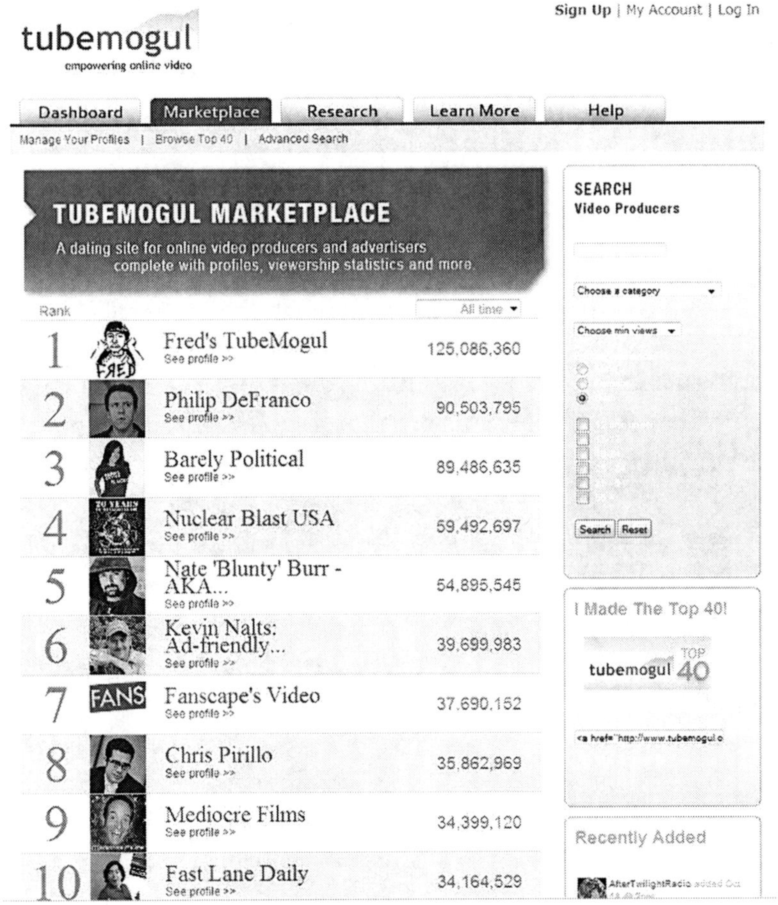

FIGURE 6-7: TUBEMOGUL'S MARKETPLACE SERVICE CONNECTS VIDEO PRODUCERS WITH ADVERTISERS.

LEVERAGING YOUR VIDEOS

Once you've built a YouTube presence, your videos can lead to other revenue streams. You may never choose to sell anything associated with your videos, but there are less direct ways of earning a buck from the content you produce. Once you achieve a level of success, you may become a consultant, for example. Jay Grandin and Leah Nelson, of Giant Ant Media, were each pursuing entirely different paths in life when they struck it big with their *How to Shower* video. Now they operate a company helping others create successful YouTube videos. That's only one way to leverage what you do. Let's consider this whole area for a moment.

Consulting

A remarkable number of the successful YouTube entrepreneurs we've spoken with are consulting with others who'd like to achieve equal success. And they are earning good money at it. This first generation of entrepreneurs didn't even have to advertise its services much. Blendtec's *Will It Blend?* campaign, for example, generated lots of publicity for the company. The *New York Times* featured the company and its entertaining videos. So did the *Wall Street Journal, TV Week, Advertising Week,* and *Business Week.* Some of the millions of people who read about Blendtec then contacted the company for advice and help. When we asked Blendtec's George Wright if it was true that *Will It Blend?*'s success led to video work from other companies, he said, "Yes, isn't that great? Here's the irony. If you go out and produce content, people see us that way and want to associate themselves with us. We're happy to do that. We've created videos for quite a few entities from radio stations to craft booking to mirror replacement. Most recently we had Nike here filming a video for a new shoe. My understanding is that Nike will be using the video for online promotion and possibly for some point-of-sale types of advertising. Also we have filmed videos for companies like Novell, eD-fm radio in Albuquerque, Altiris, and more." Wright said that Blendtec even set up a special place on its WillItBlend.com microsite for the companies with whom they work. "You can see most of these videos on WillItBlend.com under Friends of WillItBlend?" he said. "There are actually three pages of videos."

Naturally, with the industry growing more competitive, the number of companies that consult will grow exponentially. Then you'll need to market yourself more aggressively. Don't forget your Channel page for directing people to your Web site or microsite, where you can provide details about how you can help them.

Ocean City, Maryland: Gone in a Billion Years

MGH, Inc. is a Baltimore-based public relations and marketing firm with a great attitude. The company, founded in 1995, is all about fun for both its clients and its employees. This positive attitude led the group to create a very successful YouTube advertising campaign for Ocean City, Maryland, starring none other than the resort town's mayor, Rick Meehan (see Figure 6-8). A brief mention in the *New York Times* led to a brilliant idea. It seems that some odd billions of years from now, the oceans will have evaporated from earth. This isn't due necessarily to climate change or to global warming. It's just a natural evolution of the planet in context with the rest of the solar system.

But, in the meantime, let's not miss a chance to enjoy the ocean and Ocean City, Maryland, while we still can! MGH thought this advertising approach would be perfect for Ocean City, a town that sports the motto "More Fun Here." So they approached the mayor with the idea of presenting a very straightforward and sincere appeal to tourists to come while they can still enjoy the place. He was eager to sign on.

FIGURE 6-8: OCEAN CITY MAYOR RICK MEEHAN IMPLORES YOU TO COME VISIT HIS RESORT BEFORE IT'S TOO LATE!

Not only did the firm post the video on YouTube, but they also bought advertising on all the major affiliate stations from Richmond, Virginia, to New York City. They ran the ads very briefly, just over the weekend early in the summer season of 2008. Before they launched any of these efforts, they approached their "Friends of Ocean City" group to start building word-of- mouth (WOM) coverage. They started this effort on Friday, and by Sunday when the video aired, it had already had 4,000 views. By Monday afternoon, with newspapers and TV, they'd only received 6,000 views. But by Wednesday, the Fox News Web site featured it on the home page and things really took off. It was picked up again by the *Washington Post* and *The Drudge Report*. The initial media buy paid off beyond expectations.

Why was this campaign so successful? "It's unexpected," said Crystalyn Stuart, WOM services director for MGH, "in this day and age to see a politician do something like this. We knew it was also the beginning of the summer season. It's different, fun, innovative, and very short-lived over just the weekend." Ocean City has its own channel on YouTube at www.MoreFunHere.com. As a follow-up to this promotion, MGH is building a contest to respond to this first video with other videos that encourage tourists to show "What will you miss when it's gone?"

Raising Capital

Success begets success, and YouTube exposure helps legitimize start-ups, making it easier for them to raise venture capital—just stop for a minute to recall the success that came to Realvibez's David Mullings. In addition to that, YouTube has made it a special point to court nonprofits and welcome them to its site with open arms. "Video is very good for fund-raising," says TubeMogul's David Burch. The company has worked with Greenpeace and the International Fund for Animal Welfare, among others, and will barter with "nonprofits and struggling filmmakers."

Our Lady of Refuge provides one example of how a nonprofit can use YouTube to raise money. The New York–based church posted a video about its old pipe organ that desperately needed to be restored. Thousands of people responded to the video from all over the world, and $20,000 poured in. Aside from religious entities and businesses, individuals have also raised money on YouTube including cancer patients and would-be college students.

Sometimes, for-profit video production companies such as Render Films will work with nonprofits to help them get up and running on YouTube. Render has worked with a hospital, for example, to help it raise funds for kids with cancer through YouTube videos. They also worked with the patients themselves to help them create their own videos.

YouTube's Nonprofit Program

Greenpeace, Friends of the Earth, the Anaheim Ballet, the AS-PCA, all these organizations and many more know YouTube's power to help companies raise funds (see Figure 6-9). As evidence of how seriously YouTube takes its mission to help good causes, it has an entire program just for companies seeking to raise money through the site, with premium branding and inclusion of the videos in its "promoted videos" areas. If you're a nonprofit, what a great opportunity YouTube provides for you not only to *tell* potential contributors your story but also to *show* them what you're about and what you've accomplished. To participate as a nonprofit entity, you must meet the following criteria:

- You must be a nonprofit based in the United States with IRS 501(c)(3) tax status.

- Your organization may not be of a religious or political nature.

- You may not be primarily a lobbyist for political or policy change.

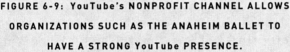

FIGURE 6-9: YouTube's **NONPROFIT CHANNEL ALLOWS ORGANIZATIONS SUCH AS THE ANAHEIM BALLET TO HAVE A STRONG** YouTube **PRESENCE.**

Further, YouTube notes that the following types of organizations are ineligible for the program: "commercial organizations, credit-counseling services, donation middleman services, fee-based organizations, and non-profit portals."

But if you do qualify for the program, YouTube can provide a lot of help. For example, it offers the following suggestions for those looking to raise funds:

- Partner Up. Find other organizations on YouTube with missions similar to your own, and discuss ways you can promote one another.

- Spread Your Message. Use your supporters to help spread your videos by having them circulate links and embed the videos themselves on websites and blogs.

- Be Genuine. Provide content that's compelling, and you'll find your audience on YouTube. Don't worry about trying to come off as "hip."

YouTube also recommends that, as the video creator, you make it as easy as possible for people to donate by signing up for a Google Checkout merchant account. (Like PayPal, Google Checkout enables people to pay merchants via credit card without having to directly share sensitive information.) You can even specify donation amounts, and then include a Donate button on your profile and all of your video pages. For more information on this program, go to www.youtube.com/nonprofits.

Joining Affiliate Programs: Amazon's Your Video Widget Program

Amazon has a new affiliate program—Your Video Widget—that makes it easy for you to incorporate product links and product pop-ups for Amazon products right in your videos. When people follow the links to Amazon's site and buy things, you earn referral fees. To be eligible to participate, you have to first join the (free) Amazon Associates program. While Amazon says you can "use Your Video Widgets to make your videos more interesting, informative or entertaining by adding product links to them," let's be honest, it's not as simple as that. The idea is to blend the links as seamlessly as possible into your videos. Otherwise, they can appear out of nowhere or are tacked on. For more information go to https://widgets.amazon.com/Amazon-Your-Video-Widget/list/. Here's just one more thing to consider: if Amazon has such a program, you can be sure that other companies like it will soon follow Amazon's example.

Repurposing Your Videos

We always believed in the adage that a penny saved is a penny earned. So if you repurpose an existing video and, as a result, save some on your marketing costs, isn't that the same as earning that money? Many of the companies we've spoken with use their videos for purposes other than those they originally planned for. These include Acadian Ambulance and Blendtec. We're all about recycling. If you can make something once and use it in multiple ways, you're saving and earning money!

PROMOTIONAL SPONSORSHIPS

More and more companies are attaching their names to online video content, through direct sponsorship or product placement deals. These "customized branded-content opportunities," as Fast Company has referred to them, have injected much-needed cash into the coffers of some video content producers.

Michael Eisner's *Prom Queen*

As an example of what can happen at the high end, consider *Prom Queen* (www.youtube.com/user/promqueentv), the first series from former Disney CEO Michael Eisner's video production company, Vuguru. (*Vuguru* is just a made-up word that Eisner thought was cool.) *Prom Queen*, featured in Figure 6-10, appeared on YouTube as well as other video-sharing sites. Its first season included 80 episodes that ran for 90 seconds each. By any measure it was a success, drawing more than 20 million viewers overall. A pre-roll before each Webisode announced that the show was sponsored by the movie *Hairspray*. Product placements for POM Wonderful and Fiji

**FIGURE 6-10: MICHAEL EISNER'S PROM QUEEN SERIES
HAS BEEN A HIT ON YouTube.**

Water also helped the series generate money for Vuguru. "Financially, it worked," Eisner told the *Washington Post*. He didn't say exactly what the company earned, but he reported that it didn't lose money, which was more than he had hoped for from his first foray into online video shows. "This is not what we expected. We committed to it with no anticipation of any revenue." Eisner must have grown even more enthusiastic, as just a few months later he launched his next online video series, *The All-For-Nots*, about an indie rock band. Chrysler and Expedia signed on to sponsor this show; plans called for their products to be blended into the plot.

Now few of us have the resources and connections of a Michael Eisner. As the *New York Times* reported, "most of his rivals … must labor to woo big-name advertisers to their untested Web content." But it's encouraging that the smart money has entered this field, and it's instructive to consider how his video company is earning money, making deals, and looking ahead.

One of the best-known sponsorship deals was between Stride gum and Matt Harding. Matt made a name for himself as the dancing guy in a series of videos he originally posted to his own site, just for his friends and family. Matt's pretty entertaining, though, and viral madness ensued. Stride gum soon paid Matt to go around the world doing his crazy dance everywhere he went, including Bolivia, Belize, Australia, and 33 other locations! The resulting video, *Where the Hell is Matt?*, has been viewed more than 11 million times on YouTube. Matt has done well enough so that he has his own little corner of the Stride Web site, www.stridegum.com, which features the original video he did for the company and several more. Another example of a successful pioneer linking up with a corporate partner is Dr. Pepper's production of a music video by our *Chocolate Rain* friend Tay Zonday.

Back to earth, Realvibez, operated by David Mullings, is in negotiations to finalize a sponsorship deal with a company to sponsor its first Webisode. As of this writing, details were sketchy, but the sponsorship deal was to include Realvibez's production costs, and provide a small profit margin of 10 percent of the revenues generated. If it were to pay off, Realvibez would shoot for a larger sponsorship package for the next season.

Product Placements within Your Videos

If you're successful enough and can make a compelling enough case, advertisers will pay you to plug their products, by mentioning them or just including them within your videos. Recall from Chapter 2 the deal between Zipit Wireless and Fred. Recall, too, the *Prom Queen* video recently mentioned in this chapter and Michael Eisner's deals with Chrysler, Fiji Water, and other products and companies.

But video producers at all levels are pursuing these deals and landing them. Realvibez has a working relationship with a clothing line, 89 Clothing, and earns money when people in its videos wear 89 Clothing, when appropriate. Hetal Jannu of *ShowMeTheCurry!* isn't there yet, but told us that "as we become a known brand, we plan to incorporate product placement in our videos as an additional source of revenue."

CHECK OUT YouTube's SCREENING ROOM

YouTube's Screening Room, www.youtube.com/ytscreeningroom, represents a potential revenue source for independent filmmakers and distributors. Every Friday, YouTube screens four different films. Most of the films that appear in the Screening Room have already played at international film festivals. There is new content there as well, which is where the revenue opportunity part of this comes into the picture (so to speak). YouTube is widely rumored to be paying for that original content. (Because expensive ads appear on that page, this is most likely true. Exposure alone wouldn't satisfy most of these filmmakers, who probably have already achieved some measure of success.) When we entered the Screening Room, one of the featured films was *Ascension*, which had won the Best Film Award at the 2008 Sci Fi Film Festival.

As you can see from Figure 6-11, the Screening Room part of YouTube has its own look and feel. In fact, it looks like another site

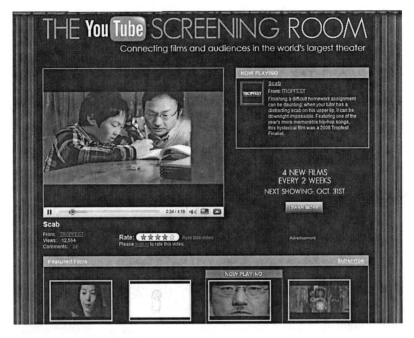

FIGURE 6-11: YouTube's SCREENING ROOM HAS A UNIQUE LOOK AND FEEL.

entirely except for all of that YouTube branding. You must watch the video in the Screening Room with the special video player featured there, which ensures the highest-quality viewing. If you're an independent filmmaker or distributor, you may want to follow up with YouTube for further information. Send an e-mail with your inquiry to ytscreeningroomyoutube.com.

YouTube's COMPETITORS WANT YOU

YouTube has spawned a lot of competitors such as Revver, Metacafe, and Flixya. They have mined YouTube to see who's popular and then made overtures to some of its biggest stars with the promise of generous revenue-sharing deals. This tactic worked especially well in the days before YouTube had its own such program in place. Revver is especially aggressive, paying as of this writing 50 percent of any ad revenue that its contributors' videos generate. Not surprisingly, YouTube has lost some heavy hitters to these sites. These include LonelyGirl15, and the comedians known as Smosh. We'll explore working with other sites in Chapter 7.

ASSESSING THE EFFECTIVENESS OF YOUR VIDEOS

By now you're undoubtedly inspired and ready to earn some real money from your videos. To do that, you're going to have to make sure they're effective, not just in terms of the number of views they receive but also in terms of who is watching them. For example, are they reaching your demographic? In Chapter 5 we mentioned YouTube Insight and the company's new *Hot Spots* program. These tools will help you gain the market insights you need to fine-tune your campaigns. But let's examine analytics a bit more now so that you see what's at stake.

We spoke with one of the true experts in this new field of online video marketing, Heidi Cohen, president of Riverside Marketing Strategies, and an adjunct professor of interactive marketing at New York University. When we asked her about metrics for success that video producers should measure, she stressed the need for producers to first consider what their goals are. "Be sure . . . heading into the campaign that you know what you're hoping to get out of it," she advised. Among the factors to consider are new prospects, revenues, cost reductions, branding, and media attention. Here are some of the metrics that Heidi Cohen suggests that video producers track:

- *Views.* Of course these are important; it's just a question of exactly how relevant they are to you. "You can't sell someone something if they don't know about it," Heidi explained. "People don't always buy the best product; rather they buy the product they're familiar with." She suggests, however, that video producers think of views as a first-cut metric and put views in perspective. "Are you trying to reach a mass audience or a more targeted one? Who exactly is your target market? What are they looking for? Or is your goal to achieve that elusive 15 seconds of marketing fame?" Heidi asks. (With apologies to Andy Warhol, she suggested that on YouTube fame needs to be measured in seconds, not minutes.) Remember, part of what makes views grow is being highly viewed, which gets your video onto most-seen lists and builds referrals.

- *Pass-alongs.* When someone sends you a hyperlink to your video in an e-mail, there is a multiplier effect. "You want to make your video available in all the places where people will be looking for the type of information that it contains," Heidi advises. "It is a plus if these locations allow you to track views and referrals." (YouTube, of course, is great for that.) Your ultimate goal is to make your video portable, so it appears on a wide range of sites such as social book-marking sites like deli.cio.us and StumbleUpon.

- *Revenues.* Heidi echoed our sentiments about boosted revenues being only one way to measure a video's success. A perfectly fine goal is for your video to reduce your customer-service expenses by explaining to potential customers how to use your product or set it up. And, of course, there are other ways to "earn money" discussed throughout this chapter. If it is dollars you're after, one way is to host your videos on your own site, where you can sell advertising against them. From there it's a simple matter of tracking the checks that come in from Google or AdBrite, for example.

- *Branding.* This is a less direct measure to monitor. One way to do so is through surveys that ask what the viewers' intent was to purchase your product before watching your video and what it was after. Another way, Heidi suggests, is to include a call to action within your video that gets viewers to interact with your firm.

- *Media Attention.* Media attention is important because it "helps fuel viewership and brings it to the attention of people who haven't seen it," Heidi said. You can track media stories about your company and videos by setting up a Google news alert, for example. There are also clipping services that will do the tracking for you.

Don't be discouraged with results from your early videos. Remember that, as Heidi says, you "have to try a lot of times before you create a hit; this was the case for just about all of the well-known companies who eventually had videos that went viral." To see what trends are hot, check which videos are most viewed on YouTube and analyze what makes them popular. Keep in mind that on the Internet, advertising and marketing wear out faster than in other media.

And, ultimately, "on the Internet" is where all of your endeavors will reside. Once you've staked your claim to YouTube, you'll be able to branch out to other social media sites to share your videos with even more people. YouTube is certainly the giant here, but many of the other sites hosting videos, although smaller, are also more tightly targeted. You may find that your fame and fortune lie not only on YouTube but also on destinations beyond. Chapter 7 will help you see where else your quest for cash from your content may take you.

WHAT I KNOW NOW

Here are some of the key takeaways from this chapter on making money with YouTube videos:

- YouTube's Partner Program can be very lucrative, but it will only be clear how lucrative once you get there.

- Exposure and revenues can be increased through a microsite or landing page.

- Video advertising can provide another source of revenue.

- Success on YouTube can lead to consulting jobs and other opportunities.

- Success on YouTube comes in many forms: reducing customer service costs, boosting branding efforts, and, of course, bringing in revenue.

- YouTube is a great place for nonprofits to get the word out.

JUST FOR FUN

Here are some more YouTube videos we've enjoyed:

- *Dog Laughing Hysterically: Laughing Sounds Added*

- *Frozen Grand Central*

- *Funny Hamster—Hamster Dance*

- *Gummy Bear Song (Funny)*

- *A Tribute to Vincent Van Gogh*

- *Urban Ninja*

7

OTHER VIDEO-SHARING SITES AND THE FUTURE OF YouTube

There are a number of video-sharing sites other than YouTube. This chapter looks at some of them and shows how you can earn money from them. You'll see that some of these sites are very similar to YouTube in that their range is broad and wide and includes just about any topic. Others, however, may surprise you in how narrow a niche they mine. But they all represent opportunities for you to earn money with online video.

We'll close with YouTube and examine what lies ahead for the world's most popular video-sharing site. That will help you plan and prepare for your future success, too.

"The reality is, if someone hears about a video they don't wonder what site it's on, they just go to YouTube," content producer James DiStefano of Super Deluxe recently told a writer for the business Web site FastCompany.com But James probably didn't have to tell you that. When it comes to online video-sharing sites, it seems there's YouTube and really nothing else. You can't be blamed for thinking that way, right now. But, as you can see from Figure 7-1, there are actually lots of other video-sharing sites, some of which are quite popular. While these sites may not get the traffic that YouTube does, video content producers face less competition on these sites, so exploring them will be well worthwhile.

Having so many potential video sites to work with shouldn't intimidate you. By the time you're ready for them, the work you'll have to do uploading files, identifying them, creating tags, and so forth will be second nature to you. And, as mentioned in Chapter 5, TubeMogul has a free service available that allows you to upload your file to as many as 12 sites at once.

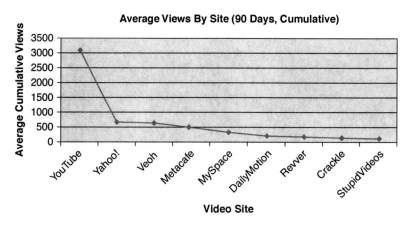

FIGURE 7-1: AVERAGE VIEWS BY SITE (COURTESY
OF TUBEMOGUL).

BROAD COVERAGE SITES

Figure 7-1 provides just a brief peek into the vast universe of video-sharing worlds. This is a universe with many planets, only a few of which can be explored here. We'll stick with sites that will give you the most bang for your buck, either because of the number of people they attract or because of their revenue-sharing policies. Revver, for example, will give you 50 percent of the advertising dollars your videos earn.

First, we'll look at the sites that are most like YouTube. They feature videos without any boundaries limiting content to specific subjects, and mostly host videos that are uploaded voluntarily, and not as part of a Hollywood-type deal.

The techniques discussed previously (for example, driving viewers to your microsite through hot links placed on Channel pages, or having Web addresses to your site appear in your videos) will work for you no matter where you post videos. Because YouTube is the market leader, having your videos on other sites will expose them to fewer people. But if you are appealing to a niche market, having your videos on a more-focused site may actually yield better results because you've better targeted your market.

Yahoo! Video

Yahoo! modestly describes its YouTube-like video-sharing portal, Yahoo! Video (http://video.yahoo.com/), as "the perfect pop-culture mashup, the best of the best." It also claims to be the most frequently updated video site on the Web, although we're not sure what they mean by that, as YouTube clearly has many more videos and updates them often. What kind of videos will you find on Yahoo! Video? Yahoo! says that they have "unicorns, chipmunks, ninjas, cats, and robots." There are also "music videos and news, sports, autos, comedy, TV clips, and movie previews." As with

YouTube, anyone can upload content to Yahoo! Video as long as the material meets Yahoo!'s family-friendly guidelines that prohibit racism, nudity, graphic violence, and so on.

If you're familiar with YouTube, you'll find yourself right at home on Yahoo! Video. The site has many YouTube-like features including the equivalent of channels—called "networks"—where you can include a link to your Web site. You can create playlists and view, rate, and review videos. To earn advertising money from your Yahoo! videos, check into the company's APT Digital Ad Platform. Its purpose is to help advertisers choose the best vehicles for their promotions and hone in on the audiences they are trying to reach "while enabling publishers to better monetize their content as well as making better connections across the Web," according to the site. The relatively new program sounds promising, although at the time of this writing the program was too new to clearly assess its effectiveness. One specific goal Yahoo! has in mind for APT is to allow publishers to manage their own networks, which to us sounds a lot like revenue sharing. Yahoo!'s Jerry Yang told *Business Week* that APT is a "big bet" for the company, and he termed it the "next generation of advertising." We have high hopes for this platform. For more information about APT, go to http://apt.yahoo.com.

AOL Video

AOL Video (http://video.aol.com/) has a lot of premium content from well-known media companies such as ABC, CBS, ESPN, Bravo, CMT, Fox, and NBC. So you can expect to find music videos, news clips, movie trailers, and full-length TV shows on the site. AOL Video does permit individual users to upload content. And, interestingly, they also have channels for other video-sharing sites such as YouTube, Metacafe, Revver, and MySpace. AOL Video seems to be another way for AOL to share revenue from Google by including lots of sponsored link text ads alongside videos. AOL Video also has a close relationship with the Flip video people. Anyone can upload to a special part of the AOL Video site at http://uncutvideo.aol.com. Given AOL's reach, you should make sure your videos appear on their site.

MySpace

With more than 75 million unique visitors watching roughly 400 million streaming videos per month, MySpace (/www.myspace .com/) and the videos on their site get a lot of attention. A great way to tap into this market is to upload videos to your own MySpace page, to gain exposure and push people to your microsite. But the hottest video action on the site is on MySpaceTV—"the video destination for the MySpace community," as the company calls it. MySpaceTV attracts a younger-than-average demographic, and its viewers are three times more likely than the online average to be 18 to 34. You can create your own video channel on MySpaceTV, and add video to profiles with a single click. You can also embed videos to bulletins that you send to all of your MySpace contacts simultaneously. About 80,000 videos are uploaded every day.

To serve this prime demographic, MySpace has cut deals with scores of content partners, some of them notable ones such as Warner Brothers and the *New York Times*. Others are less familiar such as VBS.tv, LX.TV, and JustForLaughs. No one is laughing, however, at how popular some of its shows are. For example:

> *Prom Queen:* The series garnered more than 8.6 million video streams, 90 percent of which were watched to the end. Viewers left 15,000 comments for the series.

> *Sony Minisodes*: MySpace reports in less than a week and with only two days of on-site promotion, *What's Happening?* was streamed 240,000 times; *Different Strokes,* 350,000 times. This channel has gotten more than three million views as we write this.

> *Roommates*: This site received almost four million views in three weeks.

Quarterlife (from the creators of *30-something*), was streamed more than 100,000 times in the first 12-hour period after it went live.

The *Onion*-branded channel received more than a million views, as have other partner channels, CelebTV and Kush TV.

For further information on MySpaceTV, go to www.myspacetv.com.

Metacafe

Metacafe (www.metacafe.com/) is a video-sharing site with a model that works. It's now the third leading video-sharing site, with nearly 38 million unique visitors as of August 2008, sporting a year-to-year growth rate of 37 percent. Its focus is on "short-form" entertainment, and it has a base of hundreds of thousands of videos. (The company defines *short-form* as the third leg of the video entertainment stool, taking its place among TV and movies, both "long forms.") Unlike some other sites, Metacafe is totally upfront about its deals with video creators, including the well-known producer Steven Bochco, and lots of lesser-known companies such as aniBoom, Comedy.com, Comedy Time, GamePro Media, Howcast, and YoungHollywood.com. Unabashed, Metacafe's CEO, Erick Hachenburg, has said that the company "offers producers the most inclusive and lucrative payment program in the online video industry."

Through its Producer Rewards program, Metacafe pays content creators $5 for every 1,000 views of their video clips on Metacafe.com. In return, the creators grant Metacafe the nonexclusive right to distribute their work on any platform. The company reports that videos start earning money after 20,000 views and having achieved a rating of 3 or higher on a 1 to 5 scale.

Any short video can be submitted to Producer Rewards as long as it is owned by the creator and suitable for all audiences. Metacafe's top earners, as of October 2008 are shown in the above

All-Time Top Earners

Kipkay	$118,353
Liv Films	$44,336
Fishinglivebait	$44,192
Massagenerd	$38,979
Shootingeggs	$30,123
Reel Stunts	$29,012
Jeff3230	$28,551
Maverick99	$25,944
Spacepaintings	$24,672
Loup226	$22,540

list. Notice our friend Kipkay, who we profiled in Chapter 2, stands atop the list.

In addition to these figures, Metacafe posts the weekly earnings for all of its producers as a way to motivate would-be producers and foster a bit of competition among current ones. Arnel Ricafranca of Fitness VIP considers Metacafe his next-most-important marketing tool (after YouTube) for selling his workout DVDs, e-books, and Web site memberships.

Revver

Revver (http://revver.com/) is another video-sharing site, but with a difference: it's all about revenue sharing. Everyone gets a percentage of the money generated from the advertising that appears with his or her videos. Once you upload a video, Revver will "revverize it," meaning it will attach advertising to the video. The ads may take the form of pre-roll ads, overlay ads, and even videos that run after your's plays. Ad revenue is split 50/50 between the content creator and the company. Also, the ads are *attached* to the video, meaning that if someone shares your video through an e-mail, the ad goes right along with it. You can even share videos that other members post, earning a commission of 20 percent of the ad revenue generated as a result.

Here's a sample of the sites that the company says are Revver-friendly, meaning you can earn money from Revver videos posted to them.

- Buzznet.com
- Digg.com
- Facebook.com
- Flixya.com
- Friendster.com
- MyMovieFest.com
- MyYahoo.com

- Pageflakes.com
- PopCurrent.com
- Pixsy.com
- Singingfish.com
- TagWorld.com
- TypePad.com
- VideoBomb.com

Among the big winners on Revver are Blendtec, which has earned tens of thousands of dollars from its *Will It Blend?* videos. Blendtec has linked all of the videos from its WillIt Blend.com site to Revver, according to Blendtec spokesperson George Wright. This arrangement allows Blendtec not only to generate a lot of Revver revenue but also to avoid the expense of maintaining the infrastructure and bandwidth necessary to house its own videos. Revver incurs those expenses instead of Blendtec.

Vimeo

Vimeo (www.vimeo.com/) is smaller in scale than the other sites mentioned; it has 750,000 "members" who upload an average

FIGURE 7-2: VIMEO'S WIDGET-BUILDING CAPABILITIES MAKE IT SIMPLE TO POST VIMEO-BASED VIDEOS TO OTHER VIDEO-SHARING SITES.

of 7,200 videos per day. Vimeo provides a great viewer experience—the site has a stylish and inviting look and feel to it, with high-definition videos being the norm. Playback quality is excellent. The site also encourages community building by making it simple to share videos with other Vimeo members. Posting a video you've first uploaded to Vimeo onto another site such as MySpace is a breeze thanks to their easy-to-use widget-building capabilities, shown in Figure 7-2.

What about earning money? That's a horse of another color. When we spoke to a company rep about this, we were told:

> We do not offer any revenue opportunities to our members. That is not our current mission. If we found someone

embedding their videos onto a site with the intention of earning revenue from them, we would remove their account. It's possible that this might change in the future, but that's how it works right now.

While their guidelines prohibit some businesses from using the site's video-sharing capabilities to earn money, not everyone is prohibited. Let's look at those guidelines (the bolding that's included is ours):

- No commercial videos, which means videos selling a product or service. This includes real estate, Multilevel Marketing, Get Rich Quick, Cash Gifting, Home Business, and other dubious moneymaking ventures.

- Videos may not contain any ads before or after the video unless given explicit permission from Vimeo. Videos with any advertisements in them, regardless of content, will be removed.

- Businesses may not use Vimeo to promote themselves in any way. Businesses may not use Vimeo to host their videos if they have advertising on their site.

- **Video makers** may upload demo reels of their work.

- **Musicians** may promote their music/music videos.

- **Production companies** may promote their work.

- **Writers** may promote their books.

- **Non-profits** may use Vimeo to host videos they create.

So if you fall into one of those categories in bold, we definitely recommend you explore Vimeo. Videos that are uploaded to Vimeo look better than videos uploaded to other sites and retain that snazzy appearance wherever you send them.

MSN Video

With a slogan of "What to Watch Today," MSN Video (http://video.msn.com/video.aspx?mkt=en-us) has the mighty Microsoft marketing muscle behind it, but it's primarily an entertainment site to support the Microsoft Network, as AOL Video supports that online service. Its content partners include NBC, Universal, CBS, Fox, HGTV, Food Network, National Geographic, and Warner Music. While you are free to upload content through "Soapbox on MSN Video," not one of the people we spoke with uses MSN Video as a way to earn money from their videos. To take advantage of the traffic you can list your videos on your profile. We'll give it this much: the site makes finding what's hot, most-commented upon, and most-watched, easy. There's even a separate tab for "must-see viral" videos. Microsoft isn't being coy here at all!

Veoh Network

Veoh Network (www.veoh.com/) isn't just a video-sharing service; it's an Internet television company that delivers what it terms "broadcast-quality video." It has more than 24 million viewers watching content from the site's 100,000-plus content producers. These producers run the gamut from ABC, ESPN, Disney, CBS, Lions Gate, PBS, and National Lampoon to many smaller producers providing Web-only content.

Now here's something to pique your interest: Veoh has a "unique publisher optimization program" that gives publishers "powerful tools to help them raise awareness of their content and cultivate loyal viewing audiences." These tools include a video widget (so you can easily display Veoh videos on your site) and a related affiliate program. Be sure to join the Veoh Pro program, which is free. Doing so will enable you to syndicate your Veoh content to other sites such as YouTube and MySpace. You can also receive reports about the number of views you're receiving and the comments they have been generating. Your uploaded videos also go to the front of the queue.

Veoh's publisher optimization program was just getting underway as we were writing this. Finally, Veoh also has special programs for "strategic partners" consisting of content owners—publishers with sites or services generating more than one million page views per month. For the latest information on Veoh's partner programs, go to www.veoh.com/partner/signup.html.

Hulu

Hulu (www.hulu.com/) seems to have started as a way for NBC and News Corp. (Fox) to ensure that if their content was going to appear on the Web anyway, they were going to earn some money from it. Hulu is a quality, clutter-free site that showcases legal (meaning videos that don't infringe on another's copyright) premium content. There are no YouTube-like laughing babies or skateboarding dogs here. You'll find TV shows, full-length movies, sports coverage, and clips. Hulu has struck deals for premium content from partners such as other major networks, movie studios, the National Basketball Association, and the National Hockey League. While Hulu says that it does include "popular made for Web programming," even there they only let the "big kids" in their sandbox, such as Michael Eisner's Vuguru productions (the company behind *Prom Queen*). In case you ever climb to those heights—and we're pulling for you—here's where to e-mail for more information: content@hulu.com.

And a Few More . . .

There are many video-sharing sites other than the ones mentioned above. Be sure to also check out Flixya (www.flixya.com/), Daily Motion (www.dailymotion.com/us), and especially Crackle (http://crackle.com/). Owned by Sony, Crackle has seasons just as any TV network would and makes it a point to sign celebrities for its original content.

NICHE VIDEO-SHARING SITES

The sites just mentioned may have videos in the categories we're about to spotlight, but they don't specialize in these areas. Think of it as the difference between getting Italian food in a diner or in an Italian restaurant. The diner may offer lasagna on the menu, but it's never the same as what you'll get at the local Italian restaurant. Let's turn our attention to some niche video-sharing sites to see what they offer. You'll also find other video sites devoted to other video categories on the Web, but the ones we'll explore generate the most traffic. That is, of course, except for one ever-popular seedy category meant only for adults that's way beyond this book's purview.

Comedy

Funny little minimovies have always been popular on video-sharing sites. Think about the videos your friends send you. Aren't they often meant to be funny? And the ones you decide to send on to your own friends are probably the ones that made you chuckle, too.

STUPIDVIDEOS.COM

In case there's any doubt about its content, StupidVideos.com (www.stupidvideos.com/) comes right out and says it's devoted to viral videos, specifically "humorous, off-the-wall videos, including wild stunts, wacky animals, sports bloopers, funny commercials, and song and dance parodies." The videos come from the site's partners and also its users. As with other sites, you can share videos and embed them within your Web site or blog. StupidVideos.com does have partners, but they're a little different from some of the partners found on other sites. An example is Gagfilms.com. Their profile tells us they're originally from Fargo, now living in Southern California, and that they sometimes answer to the name of the

Get Along Gang. "We founded Gagfilms on Valentine's Day 2005. Why? Because we LOVE comedy shorts! Life's too serious most of the time, so have a laugh on us. . . . [We] hope you enjoy our flicks!" Gagfilms.com promotes its Web site on its Channel page, and on that site we learn that the company is for hire to produce videos for a wide range of clients. The Web site also features Google Ads. If you have a video that would fit in with StupidVideos.com, it's definitely worth posting to the site.

COLLEGE HUMOR.COM

The magazine *Fast Company* says College Humor (www.college-humor.com/) is profitable, and as such is "the only profitable major comedy video site." The site says it's the number-one comedy site on the Internet, and we can see why they're doing so well. They feature original videos and user-submitted videos, and they even have their own in-house production staff. In addition to videos, users can also submit pictures and hotlinks to "weird stuff" from the Web. Intrigued, we found a link to an eBay auction for the country of Iceland. They have lots of well-heeled sponsors such as Kodak, Edge shaving cream, and Expedia.

CollegeHumor.com is a true social networking site with links to lots of other sites that would appeal to its college-aged demographic, user-submitted articles, a world news feed "bringing you the news each week in a way you'd understand," a feature called Pop Culture CliffNotes, surveys, and contests. There's a Linkswap program that could bring a lot of traffic to your Web site if you're approved for the program. As part of the deal you'll need to provide outgoing links to the CollegeHumor.com site. The people behind CollegeHumor.com may look inexperienced, but they run a smart site. For example, through the Linkswap console you can see detailed data on incoming and outbound traffic, and recommended linkable content.

Be sure to read the terms and conditions of use, as there are restrictions on posting videos deemed as pure advertisements, promotional, or any other form of solicitation. One more warning: a kid (or ex-kid) could waste a lot of time on this site!

Real Estate

If you've bought or sold a house within the last few years, you've probably learned how valuable a tool the Web is for scoping out properties as well as for spreading the word about your own. We most likely will never go back to a time when you will buy or sell a house without including the Internet in the process.

REALTOR.COM

Realtors, real estate agents, or companies with related products or services should definitely check out Realtor.com, the official Web site of the National Association of Realtors. The largest site of its type, it reaches more than six million consumers per month. It has millions of property listings, all posted by Realtors. The site is connected with related sites through the Move Network, which also includes Welcomewagon.com, Move.com, Homeinsight.com, and SeniorHousingNet. This site is just for agencies and "companies," but if you fit into one of those categories, you don't want to pass it by. When you post to the site, you can customize the site's resources to maximize your brand and productivity.

Big national real estate sites are one thing, but there are a lot of sites focusing on smaller geographic areas. You'll find a good example at Nashua Video Tours, run by videographer Fred Light (www.NashuaVideoTours.com).

Cars

Cars are a big part of the shared American Dream. Most people love them, and some of us are positively obsessed with them. If cars spin your gears, you'll find lots of video to explore, and maybe the perfect neighborhood for your own videos.

STREETFIRE.NET

With about two million visitors per month, Streetfire.net (http://videos.streetfire.net/) is the largest video-sharing site devoted to cars.

Upload your videos and they will join the more than 120,000 videos already there. Subjects include muscle cars, trucks, compact cars, and crash videos, which the site reports are wildly popular. When you sign up, you're invited to create a profile of your "ride" and provide details on make, model, engine modifications, electronics, and wheels. The site encourages members to connect with one another, and suggests you seek out members with interests similar to your own. We noticed that instead of photos of themselves, many people post pictures of their cars with their profiles. There are channels and car-themed shows, and users can upload videos to be considered for these shows. You're free to include Web page links within your profile. You'll also find some out-and-out commercials posted to the site. If you have something to sell related to cars or trucks, whether it's a product or a service, definitely check out this site.

How-to Sites

Just to give you an idea of the depth of some of these niche categories, the blog Mashable recently ran a story (http://mashable.com/2007/05/14/video-howtos/) about the top 10 places to find how-to videos. The top 10! And these are all bona fide sites.

VideoJug (www.videojug.com/)
In school, wasn't it always a lot more fun to go to class when you had a teacher who could really make it fun to learn? Now imagine learning about whatever you'd like to learn about, whenever you're ready, and having a great teacher each and every time. That's Video-Jug. This U.K.-based company provides access to some excellent how-to videos which it calls "answers on demand." The videos teach you things in an entertaining way. Its tagline is: life explained on film. Check out the site and you'll see why it's so popular, with millions of users worldwide. VideoJug quite understandably has an entire page describing the many awards it has received including "Best Online Video Site."

Many of VideoJug's 40,000 videos are professionally produced by the people behind the site. However, you too can upload videos or write how-to articles as another way to get exposure. The site's researchers search the world for the top experts in their fields, and if you're selected you get your own page like the one shown in Figure 7-3 where you can include a video biography as well as links to your Web site or microsite. VideoJug holds monthly competitions with cash prizes based on views. Kipkay's video *How to Make a Burning Laser Flashlight* was a winner one month. The company also has partnerships with YouTube, MySpace, MSN, and other companies.

Come to this site to gather pointers about making a great video. Just enter "Making a Video" in the search box at the top of most

FIGURE 7-3: YOU CAN CREATE YOUR OWN CUSTOM PAGE ON VIDEOJUG TO HIGHLIGHT YOUR HOW-TO EXPERTISE.

pages. You'll be rewarded with lots of help including pointers on how to make a video underwater.

EXPERT VILLAGE

With more than 140,000 videos garnering more than two million monthly views, Expert Village (www.expertvillage.com/) is no lightweight in the world of video-sharing sites. Like VideoJug, the site aims to assure visitors that it's different from other video sites in that all of its videos are professionally researched and produced. Expert Village's staff is behind some of those videos, with the rest produced by more than 2,600 "experts" in categories from Arts & Entertainment to Weddings.

How do you get to be an expert? If you have credentials from a "legitimate licensing authority," or a lot of personal experience in a field, you only need apply at www.expertvillage.com/faq.htm. Once you've passed the vetting process and are recognized as an expert, you get your own page on the site to feature your videos and a bio box. It seems just about any company, or individual for that matter, is an expert at something. Why not share that expertise and gain exposure at the same time through Expert Village?

TEACHERTUBE

As you may have guessed, the focus of TeacherTube (www.teacher tube.com/) is also on education, with a specific goal of sharing instructional videos among teachers, schools, and students. While most video sites measure their inventory in the thousands or even millions, TeacherTube speaks of the hundreds of videos available for browsing on the site. That's okay, because, as you'll see, the site still draws a tremendous amount of traffic, and for some posters it can be an excellent way to gain exposure.

You already know the connection between music and learning if you learned your ABC's by singing the letters. Now let's fast-forward to an age that brings us both the Internet and rap music. On TeacherTube, a math teacher known as Mr. Duey has achieved the kind of success that can only be reached when new art forms and technologies are merged.

Mr. Duey, shown in Figure 7-4, joined with longtime friend and music producer Andrew Yando to write and produce educational rap music to teach math to elementary school students. His video on *Fractions* has been viewed more than 300,000 times, ranking it among the top-10 videos ever posted on TeacherTube. Although Mr. Duey is a sixth-grade math and science teacher from Michigan, he's also a rap musician. He has three solo rap albums out and has a record deal with a independent label in Detroit. His TeacherTube success has helped him promote his educational hip-hop CD *Class Dis-Missed*.

Mr. Duey

Mr. Duey is a young elementary and middle school teacher and a rap musician. Along with his friend and fellow rapper, Andrew Yando, he's combined his two passions to create rap

FIGURE 7-4: MR. DUEY RAPS HIS WAY THROUGH ELEMENTARY MATH CLASS.

songs that help his students learn math, English, and social studies. You'll find videos with rap presentations on such varied subjects as fractions, integers, nouns, and cells. He even has one devoted to core Democratic values. Dr. Elizabeth Johnson, professor of education at Eastern Michigan University, and one-time Teacher of the Year, believes Mr. Duey's contributions to education will "change education for eternity." "Mr. Duey and Andrew Yando are exceptionally talented men who have created rap curriculum that I believe will transform our schools," says Dr. Johnson.

"Music as a learning tool has been used for generations by preschoolers to learn the alphabet," notes Mr. Duey. "The repetition used in rap parallels the repetition long recognized as a powerful learning method." On TeacherTube, his *Fractions* video is among the Top Ten Most Viewed Videos, ever! Mr. Duey received his teaching degree from Eastern Michigan University. Currently teaching sixth-grade math and science at Southgate Public School in Michigan, his students agree that he's amazing. They personally awarded him the "Greatest Teacher Award."

The two partners in rap are not only making their mark in the world of online video but also have completed an educational rap CD entitled *Class Dis-missed*. Produced in conjunction with Universal Records, the album was mixed and mastered by Vlado Meller, the same engineer who worked with such rap stars as Kanye West, Run-DMC, and Lil' Bow Wow.

Mr. Duey also has his own Web site, Mrduey.com, where he sells the CD for $14.95. Mr. Duey and Mr. Yando are also working in partnership with Extreme Teaching for Extreme Times to promote the use of innovative teaching methods across America. For every CD the pair sells, they donate part of the proceeds to purchase learning games and puzzles for needy families. During a recent three-month test phase, *Class Dis-missed* sold more than 4,200 copies with word-of-mouth marketing the only promotional tool the pair used. As a result of these sales, numerous testimonials have been posted that claim an increase in standardized test scores of 10 to 15 percent and subject grades improving from Cs to As and Bs.

WHAT ABOUT YOUR OWN SITE?

Letting other sites host your videos can be simple, but it isn't all perfect. You give up some control of your content. Often the site's branding appears with your video, and someone else determines the advertisers and other content providers who share the space on the site with you. It's not surprising, then, that many companies host video on their own sites, and view their videos as a revenue stream that will only grow. Just one example is FastCompany.TV. Its technology show, according to CNET, has 80,000 subscribers and is now sponsored by Seagate.

In Chapter 5 we discussed companies such as Google (through AdSense) that can help you monetize your site. There are also companies that can turn part of your site into a minimovie studio, by fashioning an embedded video player tailored just to you.

Brightcove

Brightcove (www.brightcove.com/) provides customizable video players, shown in Figure 7-5 and related services to companies looking to deliver "branded high-quality video through their Web sites." It works with hundreds of media brands and thousands of "emerging media publishers." Among the companies using its platform are Time, CBS, About.com, Showtime, TMZ.com, and the *Washington Post*.

FIGURE 7-5: BRIGHTCOVE'S CUSTOMIZABLE VIDEO PLAYERS
WILL HELP YOU EFFECTIVELY HOST AND PRESENT VIDEOS
ON YOUR OWN WEB SITE.

The products and services Brightcove offers come under these categories: Publishing, Distribution, Revenue, and Management. Many readers may be interested in learning more about the company's tools for monetizing video through in-stream advertising. There's a Webinar available through the site, which we encourage you to watch to learn more about what the company offers.

A MULTIPLATFORM STRATEGY

With so many distribution outlets available, a distribution strategy that puts your videos on as many sites as possible seems to make good sense. This approach has led to the coining of yet another Web term: spreadable.

For Web site creators, their goal for some time now has been to make their sites "sticky." That means crafting the site's content in such a way that users stay on the site as long as possible. Of course, the longer users hang around before clicking off to somewhere else, the better. This may still be the paradigm for the sites themselves. But for video producers, *Fast Company* tells us, the current focus is on being spreadable. As a content producer you want your videos to be compatible with as many other sites as possible, which shouldn't be difficult since most video hosting sites use the Flash format. Just be sure that you don't upload your video to a site that requires you to sign away the right to have your videos appear elsewhere, and be sure you understand the copyright issue of who owns your video once it's posted. And remember, your Web site should be sticky, but your videos should be spreadable!

SEARCH FOR TOMORROW—WHAT LIES AHEAD FOR YouTube

We recently spoke with a consultant who boasted that she has been tracking the online video industry since 2005. At the time, that added up to a grand total timespan of about three years. But her boasting wasn't entirely off-base if one takes into account how young the industry is and how quickly it's evolving. What applies today may change by tomorrow, as we witnessed many times in the course of researching this book. Things are changing especially quickly for YouTube, which is under tremendous pressure from Google to deliver greater revenues. Let's look ahead, keeping in mind some of the trends we've spotted.

Interactivity

Remember the first time you saw a magic trick? Wasn't it, well, magical? We had some of those same feelings when we watched

Roi Werner, the magician behind *Interactive Card Trick*, YouTube's first interactive video, shown in Figure 7-6. In the video, Roi grabs some playing cards, and a popup box warns you that this is an interactive video, "So don't sit back; interact!" Huh? Really . . . you're told to pick a card from the six he shows you and memorize it. Roi then pastes the cards to the screen, the backs only showing. Next, you're told to click on the card that your psychic abilities have told

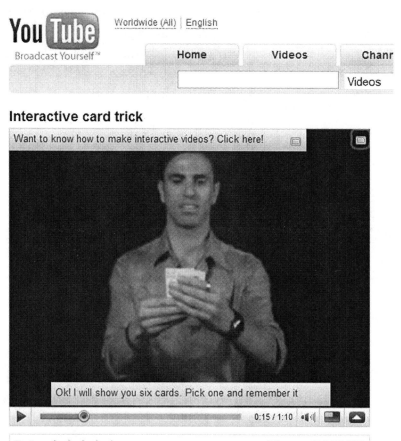

FIGURE 7-6: ROI WERNER POSTED THE FIRST INTERACTIVE VIDEO ON YouTube. HONESTLY, WE STILL HAVE NO IDEA HOW THIS WORKS!

you is yours. Roi then removes the card you've clicked on, turns the others over, and amazes you with the realization that only your own card is gone.

Since the debut of *Interactive Card Trick*, other interactive videos have appeared. The Woo Agency created one for Samsung that allows you to feel—kind of—like you're a famous disk jockey for one night. To find it search for "Samsung DJ Fantasy" on YouTube. The Agency called this "point-of-view filming." But Roi's was the first, and it got him millions of views. We can only guess how many amazed viewers clicked to his Channel page and then on the link to his Web site, http://www.artefx.net/, where there are more examples of his artistry, including commercials and music videos.

More Large Companies Will Move In

Many of the country's top media companies and other types of companies use YouTube to reach customers, boost revenues, and handle other types of marketing. But more than a few of the users of online video are making the same kinds of mistakes that some companies made when they first discovered the Web. Basically, they are not accounting for the fact that YouTube is a new medium, not just an extension of an old one. For example, you can't just move a TV ad over to YouTube and expect it to be as effective. YouTube audiences require a different treatment, but by now you know that!

A Greater Degree of Professionalism

Barelypolitical.com's Ben Relles feels that as content creators are paid for their work, they'll put more effort behind what they're producing. Consider how far YouTube has come. Just two or three years ago the site's content consisted almost entirely of homemade videos shot with Webcams. Now you can see a lot more effort and professionalism behind many of the videos that are posted. Some people contend that all of the videos that have gone viral have professionals behind them, but we can think of many notable examples where that isn't the case. Still, as the world of online video evolves, everyone will have to be prepared to create more professional offerings. That's just an irrefutable fact of life for any emerging medium.

More Well-Funded Start-ups

We've only seen the beginning of companies such as Michael Eisner's Vuguru using YouTube to generate revenues and test new online video strategies. With every new day, it seems, there are more announcements of such ventures. An example is Daymon Wayans's self-funded Wayout TV (www.wayouttv.com). Daymon, according to *Advertising Age*, is also "on the prowl for both artists and advertisers." Other brand-new companies are being formed to make the YouTube model work, specifically by forging deals with Hollywood's elite. One, 60 Frames Entertainment, has already inked a deal with the Coen brothers.

Greater Revenue-Sharing Opportunities

TubeMogul's David Burch feels that "dynamic advertising" is growing on YouTube. YouTube selectively allows some of its most-viewed video creators to host videos on their own servers rather than YouTube's—although it all looks the same to the end viewer. This allows you to dynamically preinsert ads, swapping out advertisers for brief periods of time and selling campaigns. "Some of TubeMogul's largest clients believe that's where all this is headed," David said.

More Long-Form Content

In late 2008, YouTube announced it would add full-length episodes of television shows such as *Californication, 90210, The Young and the Restless,* and *Dexter* to the site. The programs will appear in YouTube's theater-style view to ensure that viewers obtain the best viewing experience possible. Of course, YouTube will run ads against these programs and gain another much-needed revenue stream. YouTube will continue to forge deals that will provide viewers with everything they can't get now from the site, given the 10-minute time limit on uploaded videos. That will help ensure that viewers stick around instead of going to sites such as Hulu or AOL.com for this same type of entertainment. And the longer people remain on the site, the greater the chance that they'll make their way to your content, so this is a good thing for everyone.

More Monetization

You knew it had to come. Google's purchase of YouTube for $1.65 billion dollar wasn't paying off as of September 2008. Yet Google had a track record of building a great product that found a huge audience and then figuring out a way to make loads of money from it. Yes, advertising on the site, in all its forms, was bringing in some revenue—estimates were about $250 million per year—but clearly more had to be done.

With two new initiatives announced in October 2008, YouTube started making great strides on the path to monetization. Its new click-to-buy option has been especially promising. YouTube realized that lots of viewers, who watched, say a cool music video, would then toddle off to a retail site to buy it. YouTube hoped to stem the tide of users leaving the site to make purchases by adding click-to-buy links or "non-obtrusive retail links," that appear right on the Watch page beneath some videos. Viewers can buy the CDs, for example, as well as related content such as books and movies through iTunes and Amazon's MP3 Store. Of course, YouTube gets a portion of the revenue from each sale.

The monetization effort doesn't stop there. Viewers will also be able to buy video games by clicking on links appearing in relevant videos. This program is just the beginning, as YouTube announced in its official blog:

> Our vision is to help partners across all industries—from music, to film, to print, to TV—offer useful and relevant products to a large, yet targeted audience, and generate additional revenue from their content on YouTube beyond the advertising we serve against their videos. And those partners who use our content identification and management system can also enable these links on user-generated content, by using Content ID to claim videos and choose to leave them up on the site.

Global Video

We live in a global economy, so as a filmmaker it's to your advantage if your video appeals to an international audience. New tools such as dotSUB (http://dotsub.com/) can help. This software tool sits in your browser and can add captions in any language you choose. So, with subtitles, your videos can be "translated" into multiple languages.

Jumping from the Screen to the Streets

It may seem like a backward way to grow, but YouTube videos are beginning to show signs of moving off the Internet and into the real world. In November 2008, YouTube entered the real world by hosting YouTube Live in San Francisco. This was the first formal gathering of the faithful. It streamed live from San Francisco and was "part concert, part variety show, and part party," according to the company. YouTube also has promised "live performances, celebrity guests, original videos, surprise collaborations," and much more, "with the event-mixing elements of a concert, variety show and party, with YouTube phenomena always at the core." We can expect this event to be an annual one. That can only help to solidify YouTube's lofty perch atop the pop culture pantheon.

Growth Is a Given

YouTube has shown us the power of online video, and it's helped the average person gain a tremendous podium for being heard. "It has also given the small business owner a very powerful tool to market themselves. I can only see this growing," said Chris Chynoweth of DropKickMonKey.com. It only makes sense, once people gain mastery of a new tool, that that tool never goes away. It may evolve and mature, but now that people all over the world are creating videos and enjoying them on YouTube and beyond, there's no going back to life without online video.

WHAT I KNOW NOW

Here are some of the key takeaways from this chapter on some video-sharing sites other than YouTube and the future of YouTube:

- Videos may also find success on video-sharing sites other than YouTube that appeal to a broad range of subjects.

- Consider niche video-sharing sites if they seem right for video content.

- To monetize the video that's on one's own Web site, be prepared to work hard driving traffic there and deal with any hosting challenges.

- A multiplatform strategy may serve a person's goals most effectively.

- Become well-versed in the issues and opportunities that will arise from the ever-changing nature of online video in general and YouTube in particular.

JUST FOR FUN

Here are some more YouTube videos we've enjoyed:

- *An Anthropological Introduction to YouTube* (YouTube)
- *The Beauty of Birds* (Metacafe)
- *My Cat and Turtle* (YouTube)
- *Change Her World*, by Autismspeaks (Revver)
- *David Letterman—Paul Newman—Tribute—Sept. 29, 2008* (YouTube)
- *Levitation Physics* (Metacafe)
- *Dixie Chicks—Not Ready to Make Nice* (Revver)
- *I Want Six Pack Abs* (Veoh)

INDEX